Morgenthau Era Letters

119 Letters to Newspapers and Newsmakers —

Mostly in the Decade from 1941 to 1950

Protesting:

Interventionism

Unconditional Surrenderism

Morgenthauism

and

Pleading for:

A Negotiated Peace

An Atlantic Charter Peace

By AUSTIN J. APP, Ph.D.

Boniface Press, 1966

BERNARD SHAW, on his 88th birthday, about the Germans:

"Treat them decently, and they won't jump at anybody's throat."

Morgenthau Era Letters

BY

PROF. AUSTIN J. APP, PH.D.

*   *   *   *

THESE LETTERS, written in anguish and frustration to newspapers and news makers, most of them in the tragic decade of 1941-1951, some of them published, most of them not, tried to check INTERVENTIONISM, UNCONDITIONAL SURRENDERISM, AND MORGENTHAUISM. They pleaded for a negotiated peace, and an ATLANTIC CHARTER PEACE. *They failed.*

INSTEAD, Germany was dismembered, twelve million Oder-Neisse and Sudeten Germans were totally robbed and expelled, Christian Europe was bisected with an IRON CURTAIN and Berlin with a WALL OF SHAME, China was betrayed to the Reds—and America is now in a *hot war* in Vietnam and in a *cold war* everywhere.

THESE LETTERS are now published in book form to protest the continuing Morgenthauistic dealing in hate towards things German, to right where possible the monstrous wrongs it has done, and to check the appeasement of Communist imperialism, so that, God willing, the THIRD WORLD WAR which looms on the horizon may be avoided.

THEY ARE PUBLISHED in their original form

by the

BONIFACE PRESS
5353 Magnolia Street
Phila., Pa. 19144

$2.00

An Acrostic For Peace

By A. J. APP

(Date of composition lost)

THE WORLD CAN, by God's grace, be spared a third world war if Americans resolutely apply the following ACROSTIC for PEACE:

Pray—to God to make us truly willing and able to treat all nations as we in like circumstances would want to be treated;

Expect—all nations including ourselves and especially our former allies to live up to the principles of the ATLANTIC CHARTER which they all pledged on January 2, 1942;

Assume—full responsibility for our share in the past wrongs and blunders, the Morgenthau Plan, the Yalta and Potsdam sellouts, the dismemberings, dismantlings, and expulsions;

Cease—confusing power politics with ideology, such as professing to oppose Soviet Russia for its Communism while inconsistently showering aid and "red carpets" on equally communistic Yugoslavia;

Export—our Christian philosophy of society and government honestly and humbly but also efficiently, as efficiently as we now export our inventions, machines, and weapons.

PUBLISHED by

BONIFACE PRESS
5353 Magnolia Street
Philadelphia, Pa. 19144, U.S.A.

$2.00

FOREWORD

In these 119 letters, addressed at various dates to publications and public personages, TRUTH and JUSTICE are applied to Allies and Axis uncompromisingly. The TRUTH often hurts, and JUSTICE is always hard! For the Father of Lies, of course, and his mundane agents, the Communists and Morgenthauists, whom hatred and iniquity have damned to the incapacity of doing to others what they want done to themselves, these MORGENTHAU ERA LETTERS, will prove anathema and a provocation to their usual smear terrorism. But for honorable Americans they should be neither too hard nor too painful, but rather an inspiration to correct however belatedly, the frightful damage the policies of INTERVENTION, UNCONDITIONAL SURRENDER, AND MORGENTHAUISM have done — and are still doing. An ATLANTIC CHARTER PEACE must be achieved for Central Europe — and it must be done soon! The wrongs of Yalta and Potsdam have already brought World War III to the horizon — right now in Vietnam!

Though these letters were written without thought of eventual book publication, and though I would today word many sentiments differently, they still perfectly express my convictions — and are published as originally written. Not even all the typography has been rendered rigorously uniform. There is some inevitable repetitiousness. There is an occasional lack of polish, owing to haste or righteous indignation.

It has not been possible to add brief introductions explaining what provoked the letter — or if and how the recipient replied to it. It is hoped that what is needed for understanding is expressed in the letter or can be imagined. And now without further apologies, these MORGENTHAU ERA LETTERS are presented to a troubled world, like the proverbial widow's mite, in the hope of doing a little bit of good and making for a few ounces of wisdom.

A. J. APP

February 6, 1966

TITLE PAGE i
ACROSTIC FOR PEACE ii
FOREWORD iii
TABLE OF CONTENTS — Letters Listed, Dated, and Entitled iv
  1. President Franklin D. Roosevelt, Sept. 2, 1941—Neutrality 1
  2. Scranton *Times,* Sept. 14, 1941—Freedom of the Seas 1
  3. Dorothy Thompson, Sept. 15, 1941—Why Dishonestly Sponsored Intervention .. 2
  4. Secretary of the Navy, Frank Knox, Sept. 16. 1941—The *Greer* Case 4
  5. Bishop James Hugh Ryan, Omaha, Sept. 23, 1941—Un-neutral Acts 4
  6. Scranton *Times,* Oct. 17, 1941—Administration Dishonesty Re-*Greer* 6
  7. *Commonweal,* Oct. 24, 1941—Van Paassen on Holland's Neutrality 7
  8. N. Y. *Times,* Nov. 3, 1941—Negotiating a Peace for Justice's Sake 7
  9. *Commonweal,* March 8, 1942—Implications of Wrong to the Nisei 9
 10. R. L. Hatch, Viking Press, March 12, 1942—Civilian Sniping 10
 11. R. L. Hatch, Viking Press, March 17, 1942—Civilian Sniping Again 11
 12. Elmer Davis, CBS, May 19, 1942—Germany's Rightful Place 12
 13. *Saturday Evening Post,* July 5, 1942—Lindbergh and Hamilton Fish 15
 14. Scranton *Times,* Sept. 1, 1942—Japan's Rights in Asia 16
 15. Washington *Post,* Nov. 17, 1942—The Wrongs of Versailles 17
 16. Milwaukee *Journal,* March 20, 1943—The "Isolationists" Said It 17
 17. Dr. Robert A. Millikan, Calif. Institute of Technology, April 13, 1943—
       Danzig an Incident Escalated to World War by Anglo-French 18
 18. Frank Colby, Columbus *Dispatch,* July 3, 1943—What's Right for the
       Allies Also Right for Germans and Japanese 19
 19. Columbus *Dispatch,* Aug. 4, 1943—Casablanca Unconditional Surrender 20
 20. N. Y. *Times,* Aug. 14, 1943—Wrongs to Germany in 1918 21
 21. Orville Prescott, N. Y. *Times,* Dec. 29, 1943—England's Balance of Power 22
 22. Ohio State *Journal,* Dec. 29, 1943—Japanese Not Savages in 1917! 23
 23. N. Y. *Times,* Jan. 20, 1944—Morgenthau on Hanging the Vanquished 24
 24. Columbus *Dispatch,* March 6, 1944—Atlantic Charter Pathetic Fiasco 24
 25. *Commonweal,* March 16, 1944—The Pope Wants a Negotiated Peace 25
 26. Thomas Mann, Author and Emigre, May 20, 1944—Destroying Germany 26
 27. *Reader's Digest,* May 29, 1944—War Result of World War I Injustices 29
 28. H. L. Binsse, *Commonweal,* May 31, 1944—Catholics Should Demand a
       Negotiated Peace 30
 29. Alexander Gardiner, *American Legion Magazine,* July 20, 1944—
       Danzig and Right of Self-determination 32
 30. Alexander Gardiner, *American Legion Magazine,* Aug. 3, 1944—
       Is Ally Stalin Peace-loving? 34
 31. *Life Magazine,* Aug. 7, 1944—Wilson's Fourteen Points Violated 35
 32. Columbus *Dispatch,* Aug. 7, 1944—East Prussia Likened to Texas 36
 33. William Shirer, *American Legion Magazine,* Aug. 8, 1944—A *Harsh* Peace
       is an Unjust Peace 37
 34. *America,* Aug. 18, 1944—East Prussia and the Atlantic Charter 39
 35. San Antonio *Light,* Fall, 1944—German Right to Full Unity 39
 36. Henry Morgenthau, Jr., Secretary of the Treasury, Oct. 11, 1944—His
       Genocidic Plan for Germans Compared with Spenser's for the Irish 40
 37. *Commonweal,* Oct. 12, 1944—Sudetenland, Danzig, Memel—German Unity ... 41
 38. Columbus *Dispatch,* Oct. 15, 1944—Mrs. Luce on Roosevelt's Lying 42
 39. *Knickerbocker Weekly,* Nov. 1, 1944—Word 'Hun' and Eisenhower 42
 40. Msgr. Michael J. Ready, General Secretary, National Catholic Welfare
       Council, Nov. 5, 1944—Atlantic Charter Applies to Germany as Much
       as to Poland 43
 41. *Christian Century,* Nov. 5, 1944—Catholics, National Socialists, Communists .. 45
 42. Whom It May Concern, Open Letter, January, 1945—"The Future Strength
       of Germany" 47
 43. *Time Magazine,* Jan. 24, 1945—What are We Fighting for? 48
 44. Major Claude C. Wilde, Commander, Fort Sam Houston, Prisoner of War
       Camp, May 5, 1945—Forbidding German POW's Native Salute 48

45. *Time Magazine*, May 15, 1945—Admiral Halsey on Murdering "Japs" 49
46. Brooklyn *Tablet*, May 16, 1945—A Phony Catholic Committee of
Vengeance Seekers 50
47. Heinrich Bruening, One-time Weimar Chancellor, June 1, 1945—The
Honorable Policy for German Emigres 51
48. *Commonweal*, July 21, 1945—Austrian Right to Union with Germany 52
49. *Time Magazine*, July 25, 1945—Vansittart Calls Germans 'Savages' 53
50. *New Republic*, July 30, 1945—Allies of Stalin—and Franco 53
51. F. P. Kenkel, Editor, *Social Justice Review*, Sept. 5, 1945—Atrocities
in Central Europe Following Unconditional Surrender 54
52. Bishop Aloysius J. Muench, Fargo, N. D., Oct. 13, 1945—Bishops Should
Protest the Crimes of Potsdam 56
53. Brooklyn *Tablet*, Oct. 17, 1945—Winchell Keeps Speaking of "Verminy" 57
54. Dr. William Draper Lewis, American Law Institute, Oct. 20, 1945—Just
War Crimes Trials Must Try Crimes of Both Sides 58
55. Brooklyn *Tablet*, Nov. 2, 1945—Bertrand Russell on Franco 60
56. The Rev. Hans A. Reinhold, Emigre, Nov. 19, 1945—The Vengefulness
of Non-Christian Emigres 60
57. Rev. Harold C. Gardiner, S.J., *America*, Nov. 20, 1945— The Robbing,
Looting, and Expelling by the Victors 61
58. *Our Sunday Visitor*, Feb. 24, 1946—The Crime Against the Sudetens 62
59. *American Mercury*, March 2, 1946—Jews and Nisei Both Wronged 63
60. General Walter Krueger, April 20, 1946—Plea to Protest Rape of E. Prussia .. 64
61. Brooklyn *Tablet*, May 20, 1946—Barbarous Indoctrinating of German POW's .. 65
62. *The Call*, June 3, 1946—Jailing Germans for Telling the Truth 66
63. *Time Magazine*, May 22, 1946—Jews in Europe, How Many Slain? 66
64. *American Mercury*, Dec. 31, 1946—Victors Blow Up More of Germany 67
65. *The Progressive*, Jan. 4, 1947—Ben Hecht and Morgenthauistic Racism 68
66. *The Christian Century*, Feb. 25, 1947—Victors Starving German People 68
67. William Henry Chamberlin, *New Leader*, Oct. 28, 1947—Enforced
De-Nazification is a Crime 69
68. *Fortune*, Jan. 4, 1948—Wars Fought by All Nations 70
69. Washington *Star*, Jan. 18, 1948—France Starving German POW's 70
70. Brooklyn *Tablet*, Feb. 7, 1948—Re-educating the Vanquished by Force 71
71. *The New Leader*, June 16, 1948—Gideonse on Beard's Roosevelt Critique 72
72. *American Mercury*, June 22, 1948—Anti-Semitism and Feeding
Germans Arsenic 72
73. Hamilton Fish, June 30, 1948—Governor Dewey and a Slur 73
74. Philadelphia *Inquirer*, Oct. 9, 1948—Ilse Koch and the Lampshade 74
75. Washington *Star*, Oct. 13, 1948—Abuse of Germans Accused of Crimes 75
76. Brooklyn *Tablet*, Nov. 7, 1948—Anti-Morgenthau Arguments
Dewey Feared to Use 76
77. Washington *Star*, Nov. 23, 1948—Polish Oder-Neisse Prejudice 77
78. Philadelphia *Inquirer*, May 17, 1949—When is a Jew a German 77
79. London *Tablet*, July 8, 1949—Msgr. Beran and the Czech Expulsion Crime 78
80. *Time Magazine*, July 16, 1949—The 6,000,000—What Proof 79
81. *Time Magazine*, Dec. 23, 1949—Why Loans to Tito But Not to Franco? 80
82. *American Legion Magazine*, March 1, 1950—Anti-Semitism and
Anti-Germanism 80
83. *Time Magazine*, March 16, 1950—Sneer Against Just Senators 81
84. Philadelphia *Inquirer*, April 24, 1950—The U. S. and German National Anthem 82
85. Brooklyn *Tablet*, August 7, 1950—Munich Pact Prevented War in 1938 82
86. Open Letter to Protestants, Sept. 1, 1950—Catholic Church and Communism .. 83
87. Philadelphia *Inquirer*, Feb. 28, 1951—World Jewish Congress and Vengeance .. 85
88. *The Freeman*, March 5, 1951—Hitler Right in Correcting Versailles 85
89. Philadelphia *Inquirer*, March 12, 1951—UMT for U. S., Germany, Japan? 86
90. *America*, March 27, 1951—The Vanquished Lose No Rights 86
91. *Commonweal*, April 12, 1953—Morgenthauists vs. McCarthy, Jenner, Cain 87

92. *Time Magazine*, March 27, 1955—East Germany, Middle Germany,
   West Germany 88
93. Brooklyn *Tablet*, May 24, 1958—Why Leftists Make *Who's Who* 88
94. Philadelphia *Inquirer*, Nov. 12, 1956—Israeli Call Nasser "Fascist" 89
95. *Newsweek*, Dec. 7, 1956—U. S. Confiscates Alien Private Property 90
96. *Wall Street Journal*, Dec. 30, 1956—Dismantling Made Feeding Necessary 90
97. Brooklyn *Tablet*, Feb. 19, 1957—The *Bridge:* Jews Summoned, Not Destined .. 91
98. Rev. John B. Sheerin, C.S.P., *The Catholic World*, April 3, 1957—Father
   Gillis, Champion of a Just Peace 92
99. Otto A. Sinkie, *The Altruist*, April 3, 1957—Even-handed Justice 92
100. Philadelphia *Inquirer*, Dec. 5, 1957—German Generals and 'Krauts' 94
101. Philadelphia *Bulletin*, Feb. 14, 1958—Distorting a Nazi Song 94
102. Philadelphia *Inquirer*, July 1, 1959—The Inflated 6,000,000 Figure 95
103. *Newsweek*, June 1, 1960—Discrepant Eichmann Quotes 95
104. Philadelphia *Inquirer*, April 5, 1961—No One Gassed at Dachau 96
105. *Time Magazine*, Aug. 9, 1961—Nisei and Jews as "Potential Enemies" 96
106. *Wall Street Journal*, Aug. 10, 1961—Oder-Neisse Not Ours to Give Away 97
107. *The National Review*, Aug. 10, 1961—Liberal Catholics and Communism 98
108. Philadelphia *Inquirer*, Nov. 5, 1961—Lippmann Blames Hitler for Yalta 98
109. *Times Chronicle*, Jenkintown, Dec. 26, 1961—Soft-on-Communism Line 99
110. Philadelphia *Inquirer*, March 7, 1962—Keeping Maps of Germany Correct 99
111. Brooklyn *Tablet*, Nov. 12, 1962—Expulsions Prove Oder-Neisse German 100
112. *Time Magazine*, June 29, 1965—Six Million Figure Smear-terrorizing Myth ..100
113. *Time Magazine*, July 11, 1963—Expellees Want Homelands Back 101
114. Rev. John B. Sheerin, C.S.P., *The Catholic World*, June 15, 1964—
   The Story of the Crucifixion Not Anti-Semitic 102
115. *The Wanderer*, Jan. 18, 1964—Retiring Editor Giant of Right Thinking 103
116. Philadelphia *Inquirer*, Jan. 23, 1965—Hunt All War Criminals, or None 104
117. *National Review*, July 11, 1965—Baruch Vindictive Morgenthauist 105
118. *Human Events*, Oct. 5, 1965—Leftist Spender to Top Literary Post—Why? ..105
119. *Wall Street Journal*, Nov. 10, 1965—Robert Welch, Eisenhower,
   and the Morgenthau Plan 106
CONCLUSION: "Christian Formula for a Just Peace" with Comment 108
BIOGRAPHICAL NOTES 109
INDEX OF PERSONAL NAMES 110

Neutrality Being Doublecrossed

September 2, 1941

President Franklin D. Roosevelt
The White House
Washington, D. C.
My dear Mr. President:

Some little time ago I saw a headlined quotation, reading, "We have a war to win." I said to myself, "Some patriotic Englishman, no doubt, rousing his people to greater war efforts. Admirable fellow — I can understand his sentiments."

Then to my surprised shock I saw that the quotation was yours, that you, the man who a short time ago became President upon the pledge that you had kept us out of the war and were going to continue to do so, that you had made the terrifying statement, "We have a war to win."

Here was the President of the United States talking as if he were an Englishman — a British viceroy!

That, Mr. Roosevelt, is exactly what it amounts to when you say, "We have a war to win."

The British and the Communists and the Germans and the Italians have a war to win. WE DO NOT. You yourself said you had kept us out of the war — and we have not been attacked since you said so.

You commit a terrible wrong when you talk like an Englishman instead of like an American. Benedict Arnold, to whom you referred in your Labor Day address, did precisely that — he talked, and eventually acted, like an Englishman!

Please, don't do so anymore. You know as well as I that the majority, (not a "handful of appeasers and Hitler sympathizers," please, note) a majority of us, seventy-five per cent of us, do not want you to make war on Germany or on anyone else. Please, follow the dictates of the people, as the democratic president you always claim to be should and MUST, unless he wants to be to America simply what Hitler is to Germany.

I know these are hard times for you. But as I wrote you once before: Do your duty as the PEOPLE want you to do it and trust to Almighty God for the rest. And the PEOPLE want you to be American, not British. The Queen of England can say, "We have a war to win," the President of the United States cannot.

Sincerely yours,

Austin J. App, Ph.D.

Freedom of the Seas Perverted

September 14, 1941

Scranton Times
To the Editor:

When the dictators of the world address their people, they sometimes tell the truth — and sometimes they lie. One never can be sure which it is. One can't believe, one has to investigate.

Lately our own government made us jittery about a supposed oil shortage. Then we investigated — and found out we had been fooled.

The other night the President declared that Germany violated the traditional freedom of the seas when it sinks British or Panamanian ships that carry supplies to the British supply base of Iceland. He said we have the right to sink any German warship that is found in waters no matter how many thousand miles from our shores which we consider, by our own definition, defensive waters.

Then he urged acceptance of this declaration upon us with the most solemn persuasive statement: "That has been our policy, proved time and time again, in all our history."

Of course, it was — for who would doubt the honesty of the President! Only dictators lie to their people!

But one man, Arthur Krock, investigated the statement. In the *New York Times*, entitled, "New Concept Ordained for 'Freedom of Seas,'" today, he describes the results of his investigation. He looked up what John Adams and Thomas Jefferson and the rest of them had declared about the Freedom of the Seas.

He finds that in spite of the President's statement, "The rights then asserted did not include that of supplying every possible form of military and economic assistance to one belligerent against another in a foreign war without molestation of any vessel, bearing such supplies under any flag, by the second belligerent."

And Mr. Krock sums up the whole investigation into the President's remark that his declaration is our traditional stand on Freedom of the Seas with the words, "The only certain thing is that the doctrine is new in American history and laid on a new base."

In short, what the President said does not stack up to the facts of history.

Sincerely,

Austin J. App, Ph.D.

(3)

Intervention Dishonestly Sponsored

September 15, 1941

To Dorothy Thompson
Syndicated Columnist — "On the Record"

My dear Miss Thompson:

Some time ago you ardently espoused the President's Four Freedoms. One was freedom of speech.

Yet in your recent column you seem to be awfully sorry that formal war had not been declared so that Mr. Lindbergh might be quickly deprived of his freedom of speech.

You say, "Mr. Lindbergh can continue to talk what would be, were war declared, high treason."

Doesn't that sound shocking even to you — upon reflection? First you want us to get into the war so that the Four Freedoms can at the loss of millions of lives, be forced on Central Europe.

Then you particularly regret that such a war has not yet been declared because, not being declared, one of those freedoms can't be abolished in these United States! Awful!

I often wonder, are you interventionistic columnists really sincere? Do you want to get into the war because Germany is governmentally dictatorial and Britain and Russia are democratic?-Or do you simply want to get into the war because, for some inborn reason, you dislike Germany? For you talk now just as you once did about the Kaiser, then called the Beast of Berlin, now known to have been not a bit worse than the kings of other countries. Will Hitler one day be so considered, too, and you columnists proven to have been simply little prejudiced, dishonest pinheads? I wonder! Don't you fear that yourself sometimes?

Don't you think you ought to find out just exactly why you want us to get into the war? Is it because Germany is an aggressor? Then, aren't England and Russia just as much aggressors in Iran? Aren't they now, honestly? And our dear ally, Russia, wasn't she an aggressor of the very worst kind in Finland?

Then it isn't aggression. Is it dictatorship? But aren't most of the South American countries dictatorships of an equally bad kind? Then it isn't dictatorship. What then is it?

Is it the treatment of the Jews? Do you remember what Governor Talmadge said about Negroes in our own dear country? Should we therefore be crushed and disarmed by a foreign nation? I think not, do you? Then why must Hitlerism be destroyed by us — by us Americans?

Is it the persecution of the Church? Did we set out to destroy Mexico because Mexico persecuted the Church? Or Russia? No. Then why must we crush Germany? Please, try to figure that out — honestly.

Because she would endanger our foreign trade? But to destroy her would cost much more, if we can believe dear old interventionist Senator Pepper, than foreign trade has ever brought us. Besides, that whole thing is a mere assumption. Would you like to die parched and shot on a European battlefield for the sake of a mere assumption? Would you really?

I talk as one who has a brother in the army — and another brother coming up. Both are losing college years. I will gladly have them die to keep Hitler out of Maine.

But don't tell me that to keep him out of Maine we must first keep him out of England. That is a lie and a dishonesty, and you know it. Every military expert of repute says that that is one of the worst swindles now being foisted on us Americans.

An army of 100,000 can defeat a million Germans over here — a million Americans in Europe can't defeat a 100,000 over there — where we don't belong. If they could, then why can't the boasted four million British do anything over there?

Please, be honest, always be honest. Think what you will. Be interventionist if you like. But be honest in your arguments and in your statements. Don't say the Germans have no right to sink an American ship in the Red Sea. That's a lie. Don't talk as if bombing Berlin were a deed of glory but bombing London a blast of barbarism. To do so is to be dishonest. Don't say that German submarines have no right to torpedo British ships near Iceland, but British submarines are angels of the deep when they torpedo German ships off the coast of France. Be honest — Be rigorously honest. These are hard times. A lie will look awfully black a few years from now. I remember such lies from the last war. Before it is too late, start being honest and level-headed now!

Sincerely yours,

Austin J. App, Ph.D.
Head, English Department
University of Scranton
Scranton, Pa.

The GREER Incident and Official Deception

September 16, 1941

My dear Mr. Knox:

In your speech last night to the American Legion you complained that the America First Committee was more inclined to believe the German submarine commander than the commander of the GREER. I don't know whether the Committee doubted the word of the Commander of the GREER, as you say.

I think rather it doubted your word and the President's, not the word of the Commander of the GREER.

If you remember, once before, that time upon your own admission, it was the American destroyer that upon hearing a submarine beneath, and without being attacked, dropped depth charges. Therefore an American destroyer in any event did the first shooting — a horrible thing, when it is considered that the majority of Americans want to stay out of the war — and that Congress alone should order the shooting.

That you seem to have very little conscience about shooting, your last night's speech again proves. In view of all this, I think anybody would be inclined to believe the German submarine commander rather than you or the President upon that incident.

There is an old proverb: Once a liar always one.

Now you and the President have certainly not been honest with the American people all along. In his Thursday speech the President said his new shoot first orders were the traditional American Freedom of the seas policy. Arthur Krock, investigating this policy, finds that it is NOT the traditional doctrine. He says: "The only certain thing is that the doctrine is new in American history and laid on a new base." And I know history, too, and I know that this is just one more instance of the President's lying to the American people.

His end and purpose are no doubt good in his own mind: to get us into this war. But he has no right to lie to us to do it. Nor have you. The end does not justify the means.

And most of all, don't get into a dither when we doubt you. In international matters the President and you and Secretary Stimson are almost as opportunistic and as dishonest as you call Hitler — and I am sure you realize that. But I still hope that the American people will not be lied to as readily or as long as the German people.

Cordially yours,

Austin J. App, Ph.D.

Un-Neutral Acts of Administration

September 23, 1941

Most Rev. James Hugh Ryan
Bishop of Omaha
2507 Cass Street
Omaha, Nebraska
Your Excellency:

In an account of an address of yours, carried in the New York Times, I was glad to see that you seemed to prefer peace to war. After Bishop Hurley's sad pronouncement one tends to become a little fearful that perhaps other bishops have in the strain and stress of the times forgotten that "Peace on earth to men of good will" and "Sheath the sword" are the distinctive notes of Christianity.

I was therefore happy to note that you still value peace and are, I hope, willing to pay at least a fraction as much for peace as others are willing to pay for war.

But it seems to me in commending the peace record of the present administration you somewhat too charitably overlooked several belligerent acts.

You say that the administration's peace record "is beyond cavil or criticism" (N. Y. Times, Set. 23, 1941).

But I am sure, when you said that, you did not advert for the moment to our giving a whole war fleet of fifty destroyers to one belligerent against another. Surely that is a shameful invitation to war — one which we would never have tolerated from any government as meekly as Germany tolerated it from us. In that case at least it is Germany who seemed to know how to turn the other cheek. Contrast that attitude with ours when two torpedoes were alleged to have been fired at one of our destroyers. Our government was immediately aroused to risk all of its destroyers and thousands of men to avenge itself on a torpedo that had missed.

Then again, can it possibly be considered a record of peace to supply one belligerent with bombers and bombs — free? Surely it can't.

Can anyone possibly call the repairing in our shipyards of the battleships of one belligerent a policy of peace? Does this not give Hitler the perfect right to blow up anyone of our shipyards, the complete ethical right? Yet we let our government wail when he merely fires a torpedo at one of our destroyers which is doing what it should not do anyway — aiding one belligerent virtually.

No, our government, while talking peace before election, has done everything it could do to get us into war. It has done so with a degree of dishonesty and hypocrisy that seems to have taken lessons from Hitler and Stalin.

But that is not what I want to write you about. What I really should like to do is enlist your support of a n e g o t i a t e d p e a c e.

To me it is appalling that men who for years have talked about arbitration in disputes and who have extolled negotiation over fighting everywhere should suddenly be set against a negotiated peace.

Good God, is it ethical to want to completely smash an opponent before granting him some sort of peace? Can that possibly be ethical? Yet many on the Allied side, including Churchill and Roosevelt, talk as if it were. Not even Hitler is as barbarous as that. He granted France an armistice before she was completely smashed. He has again and again given indications that he would welcome peace negotiations.

But the holy crusaders on the democratic side talk of smashing everything to bits before they will have peace.

Of course, a negotiated peace will not mean complete satisfaction for us. But that is why it is a negotiated peace. It won't mean complete satisfaction for the others either. It seems that while we talk as if we had to fight against dictators it is really we who want to DICTATE, not democratically negotiate, a peace. That is the vilest form of dictatorship.

Just because we can't get exactly what we want by negotiating a peace, we rather let another million men die and a hundred thousand homes burn and a thousand ships sink in order to satisfy our desire to DICTATE a peace. Has a dictated peace ever worked in the whole course of history? It has not. Why are we so presumptious as to think we can dictate one that will? Especially since having tried so once we have failed more miserably than anybody ever did. Could Hitler possibly do as badly as we did in 1918?

You, Excellency, you have tremendous influence. I beg you to use it for what your best judgment of years ago told you as right — negotiation — for what your better sense years from now will again tell you to have been right — negotiation. The Catholic Church will earn the country's undying gratitude if it can help to bring this war to a close before we are in, before in perhaps ten or twenty years of conflict our entrance will have made the destruction, not less, but tenfold larger. Please, use your dignity and influence to encourage peace negotiations.

Respectfully yours,

Austin J. App, Ph.D.
University of Scranton
Head, English Department.

P. S. I take the liberty of inclosing a copy of a letter I sent to Miss Dorothy Thompson, because it represents an attitude.

(6)

Administration Misrepresented GREER Incident

October 17, 1941

To the Editor of the
Scranton TIMES:

I am glad you brought out in your editorial on "The Attack on the U.S.S. Greer" that Admiral Stark's report "puts a different face on the 'incident' than that the public was permitted to see in the government's sketchy version immediately after the affair."

The truth is, as it now clearly appears, that our administration shamefully misrepresented the whole episode to the American people. When at the time someone suggested that possibly the submarine commander was more right than the administration, Secretary Knox cried in accusing and injured tones, who could be so un-American as to trust a German report more than an American.

And now it develops that the German report was much more honest after all.

Friends, isn't it about time to put a halt to this dishonesty in Washington? Must we as Americans continue to be humiliated by the misrepresentations of our administration? The administration was dishonest with us about the oil shortage, about religious toleration in Russia, about the Greer incident. It violated the spirit of the Neutrality Law and then speciously asks us to repeal it because "it hasen't been working anyhow!"

Should we really sit back and allow such dishonesty to go on unchallenged? I beg all of you who are proud of an American that told the truth and faced the truth when other nations had "secret diplomacy" to write to Mr. Roosevelt and to Mr. Knox and to Mr. Hull and tell them that henceforth you want the truth and nothing but the truth. And write to Mr. Boland and Mr. Guffey and ask them to insist that the Administration henceforth be honest with us.

Austin J. App, Ph.D.

— 6 —

Van Paassen Questions Holland's Neutrality

University of Scranton,
Scranton, Pa.
October 24, 1941

To the Editor of COMMONWEAL:

One ancient and important truism war hysteria always tends to sweep out is, There are two sides to every question — and to every quarrel. All war propaganda denies this truism, yet for negotiating the just peace which must be the end of every war it is important.

Consequently whenever one can in the mass of anti-German war writings catch an inadvertent page that puts the other side in a more plausible light one ought to underscore it heavily.

Nothing in this whole war seemed so shocking and inexplicable to me as the German assault upon their cousins the Dutch. Yet, the other day, reading *That Day Alone* by the fiery Dutch interventionist, Pierre van Paassen this inexplicable assault took on plausibility, if not justification.

This Dutch writer confesses uniquivocally that Holland's "illusionary policy of neutrality . . . was fundamentally a mere trick to appease Adolf Hitler" (p. 217). Further he declares,

> *In those years preceding the Second World War, Holland virtually lost its independence to the British Empire. England did not look upon Holland any longer as an independent state. Britain's frontiers were pushed eastward to the Rhine.* (p. 213)

If Germany had pushed its frontiers through Mexico to the Rio Grande would we in a war with Germany crash through seemingly neutral Mexico or wouldn't we? We think of Iceland.

Incidentally Van Paassen also illuminates why there were so-called fifth columnists in Holland. He says the masses had not benefited from the wealth of East India oil. "The good life in Holland?" he asks. "Yes, for the crew that sat on top" (p. 221). The masses never had butter, meat only on Sunday and "we had one egg each year at Eastertime" (p. 220).

No wonder among those masses there were some who hoped more from Hitler than they had ever got from Wilhelmina!

Austin J. App, Ph.D.

Negotiating A Peace for Justice' Sake

Scranton, Penna.
November 3, 1941

To the Editor of the New York TIMES:

Of the several letters which answered mine which you kindly printed October 29, one which charges that my argument for a negotiated peace is really an argument for a German victory has such a dangerous grain of truth in it that I beg to explain.

One must assume that there are two sides to every question — and to every war. Therefore, there must be some little German side somewhere. In a negotiated peace that is just, that little German side must be recognized and granted. To that extent a negotiated peace would imply a partial German victory.

To discover this little German side I quote strong interventionists. Raymond Clapper on October 27 complains of "the monopoly of the British empire over raw materials which are essential to us." I say these raw materials are essential for Germany, too, and a negotiated peace must break that British monoply for everybody, including Germany and Japan. No peace is just or lasting without doing so.

Dorothy Thompson, on June 2, 1941, wrote that the postwar "Balkanized Europe . . . played directly into the hands of Hitler", and the allied aim should not be to preserve "that divided Europe, in which nations are played off against nations and powers against powers for the benefit of the wire-puller." Now, I say Britain was the chief wire-puller and her wire-pulling in Europe must stop. When Germany and Austria tried to end this fatal Balkanization by forming a harmless customs union, she and France prevented this necessary and good thing. Finally Hitler had to use force to accomplish it. A negotiated peace must recognize that because this Balkanization (Miss Thompson's word) was forcibly maintained for twenty years by England, Hitler was in a small measure justified in at last ending it by force. A negotiated peace must and could recognize that.

Pierre van Paassen in *That Day Alone* calls Hitler "the tool of destiny" for destroying "the imperialist concept of Europe. Never again will Europe be a beggar's blanket of small sovereign independent states" (p. 540). A negotiated peace would have to recognize some sort of Continental federation under the leadership of the most capable nation, as the Western Hemisphere is under the leadership of the most capable nation, the United States, and the British Isles are under the leadership of the most capable nation, England. As little as the Western Hemisphere could peacefully submit to the domination of Argentina instead of the United States, the strongest nation, so Europe will never peacefully submit to any domination except to that of the most capable nation there, which, if music, science, research have not done so obviously enough, this war has certainly established Germany.

I am afraid only a negotiated peace, with England still undefeated and America to back it, and Germany not defeated either but not yet quite victorious can make for justice in Europe. A just peace must grant a partial victory to Germany in the things I indicated. A British victory, basing myself on Mr. Churchill and Mr. Roosevelt's requirement of disarming Germany, starts out even worse than Versailles. Germany can no more unresentfully submit to Britain's disarming her than we would submit to Argentina's disarming us, even if with the help of some non-hemisphere power she would temporarily succeed in doing so.

Sincerely yours,

Austin J. App, Ph.D.

Head, Department of English
University of Scranton

Implications of Wrong to the Nisei

University of Scranton,
Scranton, Pa.
March 8, 1942

To the Editor of COMMONWEAL:

To my knowledge the most radical departure in our whole history from a basic American tradition is the enforced evacuation of all "Japanese-American" from certain areas. These Americans of yellow skin are not charged with any crime or fifth column activity. They are treated as aliens or undesirables merely because their ancestors came from a country with which we happen to be at war. Because some of them may be saboteurs, instead of finding and convicting these, all are pushed about, just as Hitler, because some Jews were Communistic or anti-German, pushed all the Jews about and, resisting, put them into concentration camps.

If bad anywhere, yet such an injustice cannot destroy the foundations of any European nation with its homogeneous population, as easily as ours. America is great largely because of its provision for taking in Eurasians to the full privileges of the glorious American citizenship. Throughout 150 years the son of naturalized Americans could boast his Americanism as proudly as a son of the Founding Fathers. Now this Japanese-American evacuation order abruptly shatters this principle.

It means that whenever the country of his ancestors happens to blunder into war with the United States, such an American must immediately feel that he can no longer c e r t a i n l y boast of his Americanism. Wendell Wilkie's father, for example, was born in Germany. According to this new procedure, he can now at any time be evacuated, (or, if he refuses, be put into concentration camps), merely because his ancestors were German, and we are at war with Germany. This is the possibility for some 25,000,000 other Americans of German descent, including Rockefeller. What kind of America will we have left if without procedure of the courts a foreign war can make all these people virtual aliens?

An unlucky twist of circumstances could put Ireland on the side of the Axis. Then by that twist all Americans of Irish descent might willy-nilly be reduced to aliens, as Hitler treated the Jews as aliens. Whether we would do it more mildly is not the point; the principle is the same! Who can continue to be certainly proud of his Americanism when a blundering Eurasian country can by one bombing attack make him an alien?

No. If a Japanese-American is guilty, let the FBI find him and bring him to book. Wrong is wrong, and expediency does not make the destruction of a sacred principle right. To indite a whole class of people because of their ancestors, merely because some of them, like some of any other class, may be saboteurs, in principle destroys the chief meaning of the Statue of Liberty!

Sincerely yours,

Austin J. App, Ph.D.
University of Scranton
Scranton, Pa.

Civilian Sniping and International Law

March 12, 1942

Mr. Robert L. Hatch
The Viking Press
18 East 48th Street
New York City

Dear Mr. Hatch:

Mr. Eugene P. Willging showed me your letter of March 10 in which you withdraw your name from the publicity list and complain that my conclusion regarding Steinbeck's *The Moon is Down* that "it is foolish for civilians to resist the invader," is intolerably incredible.

Since I wrote the review in question, I should like you to know that I can sympathize with your feelings in the matter. In these days all of us seem thrilled when anybody in Europe or Asia kills any German or Japanese no matter how.

I also confess that it took me a long time to decide whether *The Moon is Down* finally made one feel like encouraging sniping in occupied countries or no. Perhaps I am wrong and its impression on most readers would differ from the impression it finally made on me. But then I should like you to be somewhat gentle towards me — I would then be not the first critic who sized up an impression wrongly. Note that Roger Ascham thought the impression of Malory's *Morte D'Arthur* was an immoral one!

I believe, however, that what you really object to is my assertion that it is wrong for an author to encourage civilian sniping in occupied countries or any other acts of poison or petty sabotage. You object, I believe, to my characterizing Molly as a murderess in the story.

I realize that American thinking in this matter is under the stress of adverse war shifting somewhat. I try to keep myself in line by always imagining how I should feel if Americans had occupied Italy while the Italian government were still making a last ditch fight from Austria. Then I should consider Molly's act against my soldier brother murder. Wouldn't you? As a personal favor to me, I should like you to answer that. After all, you and I may meet often perhaps and speak from the same platform possibly, I should not like us to settle this matter in a fit of temper or emotion but as it behooves one man and another man.

For a fairly good treatment of this whole matter of civilian sniping and resistance before and after occupation I refer you to Chapter IV, "Franc-Tireurs?" (pp. 78-103) of James Morgan Read's book, just published, *Atrocity Propaganda* 1914-18. Here is one quotation from the book:

> ". . . the Hague conventions of 1899 and 1907 outlaw indiscriminate resistance on the part of civilians. Such indiscriminate resistance included notably: (1) uprisings by civilians in 'occupied' territory. Participants in such uprisings were liable to execution as rebels against martial law. (2) Individual sniping, even in unoccupied territory. The Hague rules protected 'populations' rising against the enemy, but disapproved of individual sniping. (3) Sniping, individual or collective, by people who later try to conceal their actions or who do not abide by the rules of war . . . was declared reprehensible" (p. 101).

Another quotation: "individual sniping was not condoned by any of the Hague regulations or war codes" (p. 98).

The Hague Conventions of 1907 required civilians who wished to participate in the hostilities to wear a "distinctive emblem recognizable at a distance," and "to carry arms openly" (p. 95. (This last provision has always been recognized.)

Now, I do not quote Hague because it is a Convention. I quote it because I believe its regulations upon this point conform to right reason and fundamental justice.

Mr. Steinbeck's intention in the *The Moon is Down* in his fervor of a hard-pressed patriotism is counseling what Belgium for example has labored for years after 1914 to deny as a blot upon her good name. Should we ever get into Burma and the Burmese would act the way Mr. Steinbeck has his "Norwegians" act we could condemn the Burmese as violating the laws of warfare and of common sense and of decency. Mr. Steinbeck's truer nature and the purifying nature of literature itself seems to suggest that, for finally my impression at last was that Molly was wrong and foolish in treacherously stabbing a man whose only fault was that his country had commanded him to keep order in a land whose government had safely fled into exile. I say again that impression is the only one which could make an honest and informed critic admit the book. On that basis I recommended it.

I should like you to reconsider your exclusion of Mr. Willging's name from your publicity list.

Very sincerely yours,

Austin J. App, Ph.D.
Head, English Department
University of Scranton

P. S.—I shall send a carbon of this letter to Mr. Steinbeck and possibly also a copy of my review. I regard him as a great writer and should like him to know exactly what my stand is.

————————

(11)

Civilian Sniping in Steinbeck's *M o o n I s D o w n*

March 18, 1942

Mr. Robert L. Hatch
Viking Press
New York City

Dear Mr. Hatch:

I appreciate your taking the trouble to answer my letter.

You are probably right in saying that I confused the poison issue somewhat — it may have been on my mind from reading and reviewing Pearl Buck's *Dragon Seed*, where it is clearly recommended and not only suggested as in Steinbeck's *Moon is Down*.

But of course between scissors and poison there is no real distinction in principle. If one is wrong, the other is.

I must say a letter like yours from a man of position and intelligence makes me feel somewhat ill. No matter how wrong an enemy seems to be, it sounds horrible for me to hear an American say we should discard all rules in our warfare with him. The work of centuries annihilated — no more white flag, no more taking of prisoners if inconvenient, no more reasonable sparing of enemy children, no more rescuing of enemy sailors if possible, etc., etc.

My God, can't people see that using Norwegian Mollies to stab Tonders is wrong, not because it hurts the Germans, but because it needlessly and foolishly exposes the Mollies to the firing squad? The Germans, who have the weapons to defeat an army of millions, could — if the attacks of the Mollies became really dangerous — shoot every one of them in all Norway in a few days. Their stabbing Tonders is a senseless stupidity — and to incite them to do it is a crime.

That sort of thing never works. The Indians tried it on the settlers, and the settlers are still here. The Anglo-Saxons tried it on the Normans for two hundred years, but the Normans stayed in England. If anything it tends to ruin those who try it faster than anything else. Heavens above, let's stop fighting the Axis with women and start doing it ourselves. Why aren't you over there dying yourself for liberty, instead of expecting Molly to do it?

I did not think twenty years ago I should ever see the Liberty-Sauerkraut hysteria again — when the enemy is a beast all wrong and we angels all right. But your letter shows we have got there again. And ten years from now we will be ashamed of it again. Till then, I don't suppose, as you say, you and I will agree. But if one of us doesn't die for the liberty you speak of (which I feel will more likely be I than you, in spite of your nasty Corell allusion) we will agree some day. Till then, good-bye.

Sincerely yours,

Austin J. App, Ph.D.

(12)

Germany's Rightful Place Must be Allowed

May 19, 1942

Mr. Elmer Davis
CBS Radio Commentator
New York

My dear Mr. Davis:

In your radio broadcast last night you said that unless we smash Germany completely to pieces before we consider a peace, the Germans will again in twenty years make another, their third, "attempt at world conquest."

I realize that in these war times you radio commentators are expected to issue propaganda. Yet it seems to me that even in these trying times intellectual integrity should and can rise above propaganda. I am a busy man and I don't like to waste time on letters and I don't write them just for fun. But inasmuch as you seem to me much more intellectually solid than most commentators (who thought the lend-lease bill would keep us out of the war, that all we had to do was talk rough to Japan to beat her, etc.) I take time out to write this note to you.

Regarding Germany's attempts at "world conquest." While you were saying that, I was reading in Joseph E. Davis' *Mission to Moscow* such remarks, written in 1937 by Mr. Davis, as that Germany should be provided "with raw materials and thereby [given] the assurance that she could live" (p. 108). Now, when we keep admitting that Germany did not have the rightful raw materials, how can we honestly say she is aiming for world conquest when after patient waits of twenty years she finally takes up arms to get these by force? How can any really honest man speak of Germany's desire for world conquest, especially when he comes from the Anglo-Saxon block which for a hundred years has dominated the world and owns most of the world's resources?

Mr. Davis, the nation that has the world's best music, science and literary criticism, simply cannot be kept fifth in the world's control of raw materials. The way to handle such a people is not to smash them but to be just to them, just until it hurts. We smashed them hard enough in 1919. Has that done any good? Not one bit. We cut our own throats by having been harsh. The very harshness has boomeranged in that in this war Germany's two strongest allies are nations that fought on our side in 1918. And if we smash them again and circumscribe their raw material rights still more than we did in 1919, then in 1970 the Germans under a new Kaiser or a new Hitler will rise again in still greater wrath and then they will have still more partners recruited from among the nations that were on our side this time. Mr. Davis, injustice doesn't work. Expediency is wrong, too, wrong because it doesn't work. That's why it is wrong. The Anglo-Saxon block will give Germany raw materials and power commensurate with its talents or sooner or later the Anglo-Saxon block will be terribly mangled and defeated. There is no other way. Justice, deep and fundamental justice, must be done, and those who try to prevent it, by force or dishonesties or hypocricies, will eventually pay a terrible price.

To say that the Germans want to conquer the world while England owns one-fifth of it and they only the merest fraction of what England owns or controls is hypocritical nonsense unworthy of thinking and honest people.

We can't throw stones until we have first insisted on full justice — then we can talk of aggressor nations. Not until then. We too kept on "grabbing" on this continent until we had what corresponded to our needs and talents. The Germans will do so, too. We can't stop it by smashing their armies. Or by keeping them disarmed. Their brains will break through with new weapons. We can stop them in only two ways. One is to kill off all their intellectuals, destroy all their universities and burn all their books — the Untouchables of India don't stir, no one accuses them of world designs! That's one way. The other way is justice. That means recognizing that the nation with the world's first science and music and criticism must naturally be given influence and raw materials corresponding not only to their numbers but also to their talent for transforming raw materials into finished products. This is not a matter of master race. This is a matter of not putting square pegs in round holes. If you expect to put fellows like Goethe and Helmholtz and Beethoven into a sugarbeet field you are in for everlasting uprisings until you are defeated or they have been de-intellectualized. Just as we must be allowed to be dominant in this hemisphere because we have the best universities in this hemisphere, so Germany, having the best universities in Europe, must be allowed to dominate there — as long as she has the best books and schools in Europe. And the same holds for Japan in Asia. And, believe me, Mr. Davis, nobody and nothing will in the long run stop that except the two methods I spoke of. You can't cork fermenting wine — except by destroying it. Therefore, I say again, let's do complete justice first — you can't heal any wound while the thorn is still in the flesh.

That brings me to your opposition to a compromise peace. Don't we all feel secretly that if complete justice had been done after Versailles there wouldn't be a Hitler and there wouldn't be a war at all? Therefore, isn't it more sensible to do now what should have been done twenty years ago rather than go on fighting to enforce a situation which in its injustices provoked the whole mess? We talk about winning the peace — but only after the other side is completely smashed. To me this is sheer ignorance or hypocrisy. If we really want to win the peace, that is make a just peace, we have to give Germany precisely the things which, if we had given them in 1939, would have prevented the war. And this is exactly what we do not want to do. Surely Danzig and the corridor must be given to Germany. Surely Germany must be given first trading privileges in the Balkans, being next door, not England being farther away — just as we insist that Canada and Mexico favor us more than Germany, since we are nearer. Surely Germany, naturally the strongest and best informed country in Europe, must be granted a natural hegemony in Europe, as we have it here, rather than France — or England. Surely, the nation with the best industrial talent in Europe has more right to colonies than any nation with less talent.

These are bitter truths. We may talk about expediency. I say the only real expediency is justice. Let's do to the Germans exactly what we insisted that England and France and Spain grant us on this continent. We fought and fought until we got that. **Fiat justitia et pereat mundi.** But the world won't fall if we do justice. It will fall, however, if we don't.

I say, let's offer Germany what is just now and, if she accepts it, let's make peace. We have no right to knock a man down first and only then give him what he had coming to him. If I owe you ten dollars I must give it to you even before you ask, but in any case I can't knock you down first and then give it to you. If after I give it to you, you still swing at me, then I can "defend" myself — not before.

We have talked compromise and negotiation for years — while we sat on top. Now we suddenly want to fight things out to the bitter end. I say we are acting very small. And I fear as I do for all nations which act and talk very small. Here, with unexampled impudence, we tell Japan to get out of China or else — countries as far from us as Columbia or Nicaragua is from Japan — and then after such impudent interference we prove not even able to keep Japan out of the Philippines, let alone to throw them out of China. And then, after our big talk, consistently losing for five months, we talk high and mighty about how we will crush the enemy people if they don't soon rebel against their governments! It would be ludicrous, if it weren't so sad.

Let's negotiate for a just peace now, that's what we as Christians should do. Secondly, if we are too small to do that, let's at least not be too small to talk like men. While we are staggering with two black eyes, received while butting into other people's fights, let's not wave our fists at the opponents threatening wildly what we will do to them when we finally get on top of them. We may not get on top — and then we will look even more ludicrous than we did when we told Japan what to do in China — and lost the Philippines for our arrogance.

Very sincerely yours,

Austin J. App, Ph.D.

Lindbergh and Hamilton Fish were Right

Loras College, Dubuque, Iowa, July 5, 1942

The Saturday Evening Post
Independence Square,
Philadelphia, Pa.

Dear Sir:

I am so much in sympathy with the underlying theme of your July 4th editorial, "Limits to a Purge," that I hereby object to one sentence in it only because it seems to express a general fallacy current since Pearl Harbor.

You speak of Hamilton Fish and some of "our prize isolationists" as having diagnosed the war so very mistakenly and hence should not be honored with trust. But surely it was not Hamilton Fish or Wheeler or Lindbergh who diagnosed the war mistakenly; it was President Roosevelt and Knox and Stimson who did so. It was the former who warned that the Lend-Lease bill would lead to war; but it was the Administration who urged and achieved its passage with the argument that it was a step to keep us out of war. After this, possibly the most criminal mistake in American history, who can be accused of diagnosing the war mistakenly — Hamilton Fish or the Administration? Hamilton Fish said that repealing and violating the spirit of our neutrality laws would lead to war; Mr. Roosevelt said it would keep us out of the war. Pearl Harbor proved whom right? And so on and on.

Mr. Lindbergh said the interventionists were winning all debates and none of the campaigns. Last week a member of the British Parliament said exactly the same thing. Who was right, Mr. Lindbergh, or Mr. Roosevelt, who called everybody a defeatist who said that England, in spite of Mr. Churchill's assertion that if we send the guns England will do the job, can't win merely with our guns and goods? Clearly, Mr. Lindbergh and Mr. Fish were right.

To say that the so-called isolationists diagnosed the war mistakenly and the Administration or the interventionists correctly is a terrible travesty on facts and honesty. The British Government said that Hitler had missed the bus, that Germans will be out of Norway before a summer would be over, that Crete would hold, that Rommel would be smashed in Africa, that Singapore would hold — and they were wrong. Our Administration, sneering at the non-interventionists, said that cash and carry would win the war for England, then that lend-leasing would keep us out of the war, that Japan could be brow-beaten by tough words into forsaking China and would be too scared to attack us — and the Administration was wrong, dead wrong, on every point. Now to say instead that the non-interventionists were wrong is a dishonesty one must not print. During a war it may not be wise to print that the Administration horribly mis-diagnosed the war — but surely, while one may be quiet about certain things, one has never the right to transfer mistakes from the guilty to the innocent.

To do so is unworthy the glorious record of the *Post*. I trust it was merely an unfortunate slip.

Sincerely yours,

Austin J. App, Ph.D.

(14)

Japan's Rights in Asia are Real

September 1, 1942
Scranton, Pa.,

To the Editor of the *Scranton Times:*

To your fine editorial of August 31, pointing out what a terribly formidable foe former ambassador to Tokio, Joseph C. Grew, makes Japan out to be, I should like to add one less black quotation from Mr. Grew's speech. He says that the purpose of the Japanese military machine is "to control what the Japanese have latterly termed 'The Co-Prosperity Sphere of Greater East Asia, Including the South Seas.' It need hardly be said that the phrase 'Co-Prosperity Sphere' denoted in fact the intention to exert Japanese control, politically, economically — absolutely — over all those far-flung territories."

The clear sense of this statement is that according to Mr. Grew the Japanese do not want to control the whole world or this hemisphere or even all of Asia — only East Asia.

Of course, it is intolerably presumptious and illogical of the Japanese to think that, just because we in the Monroe Doctrine and otherwise insist on dominating this hemisphere and send marines and cruisers to Nicaragua and Cuba and Uruguay whenever they don't behave, they may do the same thing to the peoples surrounding Japan. They forget that they are after all only little yellow Shintoists, whereas we are tall, handsome Christians.* For us to control the West Indies and Central America, and furthermore with the help of the English, who are also tall, handsome Christians, even to police the whole world for the next hundred years, as Secretary Knox wants, is perfectly proper. And naturally, if those inferior Japs think they may police the China coast or the East Indies, we must sacrifice billions in gold and millions in crippled and killed men, if necessary, to keep them walled up among their own volcanos.

Nevertheless, Mr. Grew's statement that the Japanese want only East Asia is consoling, for it assures us that, in case we should ever get tired of policing Asia and wish to confine ourselves to policing this hemisphere, the Japanese, if Mr. Grew is right, will be glad enough to stay on their side of the Pacific.

Sincerely,

Austin J. App, Ph.D.

* Editorial Note, added Nov. 28, 1965:

It was not, of course, the honorable Christians who got America into the war through the backdoor by harassing Japan, but the New Deal amalgam of hypocrites, Morgenthauists, Communists, and phony liberals. These same wretches are the ones who after our victory in the dirtiest manner stabbed Free China in the back and delivered her over to the Reds. That is why we had to fight in Korea in 1950, and are fighting in Vietnam now. These same treasonable elements are the ones who wanted President Diem assassinated and hoped and hope to betray all of Vietnam to the Reds.

(15)

Wrong of Versailles Needed Correcting

Fort Belvoir, Va.,
November 17, 1942

Washington Post
Washington, D. C.
To the Editor:

One of your correspondents declares that a negotiated peace is bargaining for another war, that "To dictate peace is to secure peace," that "Germany must be disarmed," and finally he says, "Let us learn from history." Now, ironically, if we are to learn from history, then we must absolutely not do everything he insists upon.

In 1918 we absolutely refused to negotiate a peace. We insisted upon dictating it unconditionally and we did. And the dictated peace to end all wars led to this war, much worse than the other by the fact that two of our chief allies in the last war, Italy and Japan, are this time on the German side. That is the price of a dictated peace. A negotiated peace would never have led to the injustices that drove even two of our former allies against us.

Then he says Germany must be disarmed. But again the history he invokes tells us that Germany was disgracefully disarmed in 1918 and kept disarmed for fifteen years.

No, if history is to be invoked then we ought to try justice this time in our peace treaty — real honest justice. If other nations are to have armies, Germany must be allowed to have them. If England and America may have colonies and raw materials in all parts of the world, Germany must be accorded the same rights. And if Danzig is a German city more than a Polish one, then she must be given Danzig. A dictated unjust peace has failed once, let's try justice this time. Because an ignorant, illiterate nation like India can for centuries be successfully subjected to injustice, does not at all prove that a nation which ranks with the first in science and music and scholarship can ever be successfully disarmed or treated with indignity or injustice. Therefore, I say again, let's honestly try justice this time.

Sincerely yours,

Austin J. App, Ph.D.

————————◦◦◦————————

(16)

The "Isolationists" Foretold It

Menomonee Falls, Wisconsin
March 20, 1943

The Editor,
The Milwaukee Journal
Milwaukee, Wisconsin
Gentlemen:

In your editorial of March 19, 1943, "Still Living in 1919" you are right in favoring a post-war international cooperation. But you vitiate your editorial by asking, Did the isolationists "keep us out of the war?"

That is like blaming the escape of the cow on the fellow who wanted her kept tied instead of on the one who insisted on loosing her.

The isolationists warned that the veritably treasonable destroyer deal would lead to war. The interventionists said, "No, it won't." The

— 17 —

isolationists begged, "The Lease-Lend Bill will lead to war — please don't pass it." But the smart interventionists asserted, "Oh, no, it's a step to keep us out of war." And they passed it and bombed the Japanese from China with lend-lease bombers. When finally, wisely biding their own good time, the Japanese retaliated at Pearl Harbor, the same lend-leasing interventionists set up a howl that somehow the isolationists had got us into the war, the very isolationists who had warned against and predicted the obvious consequences of the Lend-Lease Bill.

Gentlemen, don't be dishonest. It doesn't pay — not even for fighting this lend-lease war. The interventionists lend-leased us into this war. If you want a maximum of isolationist support for it, admit the interventionistic crime of getting us into it and then, "since there's no help," humbly beg the isolationists for forgiveness and support.

Remember, you can admit the truth now — or you can do it twenty years from now. But I promise you, sooner or later you will admit it. Don't be too little and too late.

Sincerely yours,

Austin J. App, Ph.D.

(17)

Danzig, 1939, an Incident Escalated into World War by Anglo-French

3860 Trabue Rd., Hilliard, Ohio
April 13, 1943

Dr. Robert A. Millikan
California Institute of Technology
Pasadena, California

My dear Dr. Millikan:

It greatly pleased me to read in an AP report that you had punctured the fallacy that war stimulates scientific research.

It only remained that you should have insisted that all nations, all large nations, because they reject Christ's turn-the-other-cheek and sheathe-the-sword philosophy, are responsible for world wars. I am sorry you spoke of "bandit nations" running amuck.

Who are the bandit nations you would have us police this time? Germany, Italy, and Japan. And who are they? Well, they happen to be largely, that is, two out of three, our former sweet and precious allies of 1918. Now we advocate policing them.

If our allies of 1918 now need to be policed by us, how can you be sure that our allies of today, dear and sweet Soviet Russia and China, and India and South Africa and Britain itself will not have to be policed by us a few years hence. Russia, for example, surely doesn't look a bit more sweet and gentle now than Italy and Japan looked to us in 1918.

I trust you see what I am driving at. Germany did not start the world war. It created an incident at Danzig, just as some years before Poland created an incident at Vilna. One led to a world war, the other did not. Why? Because of Germany. No, surely not. Because of England and France and us — we lifted that incident into a world war, just as we did not lift the Vilna incident into a world war. In 1914 Germany played the precise part in the world conflagration that England and France played this time. Austria and Serbia had an incident, Russia

— 18 —

proceeded against Austria, and then Germany, bound by treaty to protect Austria against Russia, as Britain bound itself to protect Poland against Germany, got into the war. Yet, at Versailles we attributed sole war guilt to Germany. Logically, therefore, we should now have to attribute sole war guilt to Britain. Or considering Roosevelt's Quarantine speech of October 5, 1937, which in a way put an end to the peaceful revision of the Versailles treaty, to America.

To speak of bandit nations solely responsible for the war is to make a just peace virtually impossible. It prepares the way for a bigger and smellier Versailles. And the fruit will be that some years from now we will have to call some of the dear sweet blue-eyed allies of today the bandit nations, just as we are calling Japan and Italy, our sweet, dear allies of 1918, bandit nations.

Justice, Dr. Millikan, justice, real justice for all nations, not policing, is what we need.

Sincerely yours,

Austin J. App, Ph.D.

---

(18)

What's Right for Allies also Right for Germans and Japanese

3860 Trabue Rd., Hilliards, Ohio
July 3, 1943

Mr. Frank Colby
Care of the *Columbus Dispatch*
Columbus, Ohio

Dear Mr. Colby:

I read your feature in today's *Dispatch* upon the Japanese word "Bushido." And while the article is of course interesting it also reveals a vice habitual in war — that of making unfair comments upon the enemy.

Each side does it in every war, but the more civilized side ought to do it less. And doing it at all is never worthy of a gentleman, or, I like to think, of an American.

At the Governor's Dinner recently I heard Joseph Davies visualize the ruins of Stalingrad and then denounce the Germans as the worst barbarians in history for destroying such a city. Subsequently he boasted how our Flying Fortresses and RAF bombers were making rubble out of the German cities on the Rhine.

Why are the Germans *barbarians* for destroying Stalingrad but we *crusaders* for destroying Cologne and Naples. A gentleman even in war cannot argue that way — and an American ought not.

You accuse the Japanese of many things which may be true and which we Americans probably have not done and will not do, even if we get into enemy territory. But you also castigate them for things we ourselves are doing. You say they annihilate defenseless Chinese communities. Did we not annihilate defenseless North African communities and don't we intend to annihilate a good many more on our envisaged march from Sicily and Dieppe to Berlin?

You say they bombard hospitals and churches. They do. That they do so viciously and on purpose you cannot say honestly. That we, too, bomb hospitals and churches only a dishonest or stupid person will deny. If we want war we must expect our enemies to fight it just as we fight

— 19 —

it — with the same hellish results. An American flyer over Berlin is no more or less noble than a German flyer over London. This we have to get into our thick prejudiced skulls, if we want to be worthy of the name of gentleman and, I like to think, American. For I like to think of us Americans as the justest and fairest people in the world. If we aren't that, then we have even less reason than alleged for trying to tell the Germans what kind of Government they may have and who their Fuehrer should be.

It is very probably true that the Japanese rape more enemy women than Americans do or would do had they chance. But as one who has been in this army I know that American soldiers have raped even some of their own women. They would undoubtedly rape also some enemy women were they deep in enemy territory. I am not sure that it becomes us to throw stones of that type too liberally.

An army that is constantly being supplied with rubber prophylactics, that I know has in some instances required every man in the company to have a package with him before being granted a pass, can hardly with good grace carry on about the immorality of opposing armies.

I should like you in the future to be absolutely fair. I like to think of America as big and strong enough so it and every citizen can be fair — fair even to the devil. I think you will admit on sober reflection that your article is not quite fair. Unfairness will not help win any war — but it does contribute powerfully to wreck the hopes of a decent and reasonably permanent peace.

Very sincerely yours,

Austin J. App, Ph.D.

----

(19)

Casablanca Unconditional Surrender Policy Immoral

Trabue Rd., Hilliards, Ohio
August 4, 1943

Columbus...*Evening Dispatch*
Columbus, Ohio

To the Editors:

As far as I know, your August 3 editorial, "Differences Develop in Allied Ranks," is the first in the country to express common sense regarding the Casablanca Unconditional Surrender demand.

You indicate that what with Russia suggesting negotiated surrender to Germany, and Italy having turned down our Unconditional Surrender ultimatum, we might with profit re-examine the much advertised Casablanca demand.

You say, "It is almost impossible for a nation, as such, to accept unconditional surrender without inviting internal anarchy."

You are right. Furthermore, no nation can ever do so honorably. And no later generation ever forgives its fathers for accepting unconditional surrender . . . If our fathers had ever accepted unconditional surrender from anybody we would spit on them.

Demanding unconditional surrender is both a mistake and a sin. Mr. Roosevelt said Rome had to be bombed to save our soldiers' lives. What about the American soldiers that have died from Italian bullets fired since the new, non-fascistic government of Italy was pushed back into Hitler's arms by our swashbuckling unconditional surrender demand?

And over and above everything else, the unconditional surrender demand is unethical. It is so unethical that the justice of even the most idealistic war becomes vitiated as soon as and as long as Unconditional Surrender is insisted upon.

If you and I fight because you stole ten dollars from me, I must be willing to stop hitting you as soon as you say, "Here is your ten dollars and the key with which I got into your house, and I won't do it again."

If thereupon I continue to hit you and say, "You've got to give up unconditionally — give up everything you have and I may want; of course, you can trust me to be reasonable afterwards, but now you must be willing to give up everything — all your money, clothes, house, wife and children before I stop beating you," then I am a brute and my war becomes grossly unethical.

That's what we are if we demand unconditional surrender before being willing to stop killing and destroying — and, incidentally exposing thousands of our own boys to unnecessary death.

We want the war to end as quickly as possible, and the peace to be as just as possible. Demanding unconditional surrender makes the war last as long as possible (which will make it seem necessary not to change horses in mid-stream), and makes a second and far worse Versailles peace almost a certainty — unless the Germans, as you suggest and Russia seems to desire, save themselves by going Communistic with Russia. Which God forbid!

Austin J. App, Ph.D.

------

(20)

Wrongs to Germany in 1918

3860 Trabue Rd., Hilliards, Ohio
August 14, 1943

The New York *Times*
New York City

To the Editor:

In his letter of August 12, urging that the Germans be identified with Hitler, Charles Mackay says that in 1918 we "threw away victory . . . by absolving the German people and nation of responsibility for the misdeeds of its entity."

It is curious how persistent this total error is. The victory in 1918 was lost precisely because England and France, crushing Wilson and his Fourteen points, insisted on punishing the whole German people for what, before the Armistice, were propagandized as the crimes of the Kaiser and distinctly not of the German people.

The facts are that the German people expelled the Kaiser and his government whom we had been declaring the unacceptable obstacles to peace and democracy. But after the Germans had kicked the Kaiser into Holland and signed the armistice, we went to work on the German people. First of all, we required them to accept a dictated peace unconditionally, even as we want to again. Then we brow-beat the German people and their Republican government, which we had almost created, into signing the total war guilt clause — we did not force the Kaiser to sign it, we forced the German people. Then we imposed, not on the Kaiser (who was in Holland), but on the German people reparations so monstruous that they and their children to the tenth generation could not in spite of the most abject slavery satisfy them. In addition part of the German territory remained occupied, parts of the German people were assigned to other nations, their colonies were taken away, and they were not only disarmed but required to stay in a state of disarmament. All this was done to the German people who had been told by us that the quarrel was with their government, not with them.

What further, after this war, would Mr. Mackey suggest be done to the German people? Edmund Burke said one can't indict a whole people. But perhaps one can hang all of them. Mr. Roosevelt and Churchill want to electrocute the governments of Germany and Italy. Perhaps, if as Mr. Mackay suggests, the German women and children are equally guilty with their governments, he advocates electrocuting the whole pack of them. Then surely they could not be blamed for a future war, and England and America and France could happily return to fighting each other again the way they did during all the centuries when the Germans were kept split into some two hundred starved and pestiferous little provinces, who did not do any fighting but were fought over by the others.

Austin J. App, Ph.D.

————————

(21)

England's Balance of Power Policy Catastrophic

476 W. 7th Ave., Columbus, Ohio
December 29, 1943

Mr. Orville Prescott
c/o New York *Times*
New York City

My dear Mr. Prescott:

In your review of December 24, 1943, you speak of England as "the only bulwark that stood between us and the brown pestilence of Europe." This was of course Mr. Roosevelt's favorite and insistent contention while he was destroyer-dealing and lend-leasing us into the war and it is therefore only natural that the rest of us should glibly say the same thing.

Nevertheless, since you are an important publicist who no doubt wishes to convey to the public only what is true and just of friend and enemy, I thought the following quotations on the point might interest you.

F. A. Voigt, editor of the important British magazine, *The Nineteenth Century and After,* said in the September, 1943, issue:

"England fought to preserve the balance — for that reason and no other.

"The commonly accepted view that Germany made war to dominate the world is, in our opinion, mistaken. She wanted to be a world power, but world power and world domination are not the same thing . . . Hitler would have been glad to share the world with the English . . . His main purpose in going to war was to subjugate the European mainland and then to open up Russia for German colonization."

Mr. Voigt is with good reason called the spokesman of Lord Vansittart, long England's Under Secretary of Foreign Affairs. The above

— 22 —

British statement supports Hitler's own contention that he had no hope or desire to conquer the United States.

And as for Germany threatening us, Demaree Bess in "Let's Quit Pretending" (Saturday Evening Post, December 18, 1943) says that "Before Germany declared war against us, we were unconditionally pledged to support . . . Soviet Russia and the British Empire" against Germany and were "already deeply involved in the European war, having committed a whole series of war-like actions against Germany," and "President Roosevelt had pledged us to 'overthrow Hitlerism,' which could only mean to defeat Germany."

According to these statements it wasn't the brown pestilence that threatened us, but we who came to the aid of the island bulwark in its effort to keep the Germans from becoming a world power, as Mr. Voigt puts it, of European dimensions.

At any rate I thought these quotations might interest you.

Very sincerely yours,

Austin J. App, Ph.D.

————●◆●————

(22)

Japanese Not Savages in 1917!

476 W. 7th Ave., Columbus, Ohio
December 29, 1943

Ohio State *Journal*
Columbus, Ohio

To the Editor:

Your attitudes and editorials generally are so large-minded and humane that I hope you will not take it too much amiss if I single out one word for criticism in your editorial of December 29 on the government's or army's suppression and manipulation of certain forms of news.

In that editorial you speak of "the kind of savage we are up against in the Jap."

I am sorry you called the Japanese *savages* and I hope you will not do so again. In 1918 the Japanese were our beloved allies and our Wilsonian government at that time encouraged everybody to call them all kinds of charming names.

Now that Japan is on the other side there is a temptation to call them savages. If they are savages in 1943 then they were savages in 1917. Are we going to admit that in our "glorious" battle to "save the world for democracy" under Wilson we had savages as important allies?

The Japanese are not savages. They are the most highly civilized people with the best schools and universities and the lowest rate of illiteracy in all of Asia. They are, I feel one can honestly say, not as civilized as yet as we are, but they are more highly civilized and less savage than some of our present allies.

Someday the Japanese may again be our allies and then we'll feel very much ashamed for having called them savages. What sickened and shamed the human race and us most after the last world war was not the atrocities committed by the other side, but the atrocity stories about the other side the British and the French manufactured and we publicized and believed. This must not happen again.

Very truly yours,

Austin J. App, Ph.D.

— 23 —

(23)

Morgenthau on Hanging the Vanquished

Columbus, Ohio, January 20, 1944

To the Editor,
The New York *Times*

On January 18, you reported Mr. Morgenthau's praising the Russians for "stringing the ringleaders of hate up and letting them hang there until they are dead." And you report him as indicating that "this was the proper fate for all those guilty of starting the war."

I wonder whether Mr. Morgenthau adverted to the ironic appropriateness of the Russians beginning the business of hanging those guilty of starting wars! It means, of course, that if Hitler is to be hanged for trying to get Danzig back by force then Stalin must be hanged for assaulting the Finns for a slice of Finland. I am sure Mr. Morgenthau must have been conscious of that, for Mr. Morgenthau is a good American, and Americans are noted for their fairness, for their insistence that what's sauce for the goose is also sauce for the gander. If Mr. Morgenthau's idea of punishing war criminals is correct, then we will see some interesting hangings!

Austin J. App, Ph.D.

(24)

Atlantic Charter Forsworn by Roosevelt and Churchill

476 W. 7th Ave., Columbus 1, Ohio
March 6, 1944

Columbus *Dispatch*
Columbus, Ohio
To the Editor:

Your splendid editorial on the "Charter Crisis" indirectly makes clear what a pathetic fiasco the Atlantic Charter is proving to be for the American people. In August, 1941, when Roosevelt and Churchill signed it we were a declared neutral nation and neither Germany nor Japan, though they had done to some countries what Russia had done to Finland, had done us any harm whatsoever. Yet in the sixth article, "After the final destruction of the Nazi tyranny," Mr. Roosevelt virtually declared war on Germany without benefit of Congress or the people.

By suggesting that if the United States helped defeat Germany, the world would get so fair and just a peace that not only Asia and Poland and the little nations of Europe but even the Germans themselves would be better off losing under Roosevelt than winning with Hitler, the American people were brought to tolerate Mr. Roosevelt's shoot-on-sight order of Sept. 11, 1941, against German submarines, and Mr. Hull's get-out-of-China-or-we'll-kick-you-out proposal to Japan of Nov. 26.

But as soon as the thing Churchill had "dreamed of, aimed at and worked for" had happened, when the Allies had us "in it with" them, then they began to sabotage the Atlantic Charter; it had been a raft to ride the American people into the war, and now it was ready to be scuttled.

Soon after Churchill gave his notorious what-we-have-we-hold speech and thus scuttled the charter for the millions of India and Burma whom Britain had "forcibly deprived" of "sovereign rights and self-government." Mr. Roosevelt looked on in silent approval.

When with our lend-lease Russia made some progress, she declared

— 24 —

that the boundaries of Poland and Finland and the Baltic states are none of our business. Mr. Churchill adds, "I have intense sympathy for the Poles . . . But I also have sympathy for the Russian standpoint."

Mr. Roosevelt is silent when Russia demands all the Baltic states, a part of Finland, and half of Poland. He still insists that, though we have made an ally out of Stalin, we cannot talk about peace with Hitler.

Recently, Mr. Churchill finally gave the once-proud charter its final torpedo and robbed it of its one remaining valuable implication — namely that it assured enemy peoples of a peace reasonably just enough to help induce them to accept it. On Feb. 22, Churchill said, "There will be no question . . . of the Atlantic Charter applying to Germany as a matter of right and barring territorial transferences or adjustments to enemy countries."

So the grand charter is finally scuttled. And now, the better we fight the more Russia will get of Europe and the more Britain will keep of Asia.*

Austin J. App, Ph.D.

* Editorial note added Nov. 28, 1965:

But the fact that the Atlantic Charter was calculated by Roosevelt and Churchill as a monumental fraud to trick the American people into the war, does not mean that its principles are not valid or have not been solemnly pledged to by the U.S. and Britain and Soviet Russia and all the Allied nations. We, the American people, have the moral obligation to require our and the Allied governments to grant the vanquished the kind of peace promised in the Atlantic Charter, because only such a peace is just, and only such a peace may be enforced and deserves to last.

(25)

Pope Pius XII Wants Negotiated Peace

476 W. 7th Ave., Calumbus 1, Ohio
March 16, 1944

COMMONWEAL
386 Fourth Ave.
New York City

To the Editor:

This letter is not in reference to anything specific in *Commonweal.* It is merely begging space for something I feel ought to be said. Even the pagans will say it fifteen years from now, the time for a Christian to say it is now.

The tragic part of war is death and destruction, but the pathetic part of it is the blinding of men's minds.

The Catholic University psychologist, Dr. Allers says, "Many people . . . are even willing to change, but they expect others to change first. 'I know,' a man will say, 'that I am treating my wife badly and I am quite disposed to change my behavior, provided that she first leaves doing this and begins doing that.' "

Good, ethical-minded Catholics that we are, we immediately see how foolish this husband's attitude is.

But during a war, in international matters, for which the same moral laws should hold, we complacently and implicity support the husband's attitude.

We say, "War is villainous. We hate war. We hate to destroy cities
and bomb Monte Cassinos and kill human beings. And we are anxious
and glad to stop it as soon as the Germans stop it first by accepting Unconditional Surrender and let us divide them into small parts and give
East Prussia to Russia and let us dismantle their factories and keep them
disarmed forever and let us hang all their leaders and militarists and let
us tell them how they must be governed and let us impose upon them and
their children our educational ideas. If they accept that unconditionally
we will be very happy indeed to stop this slaughter."

In the meanwhile Pope Pius XII pleads with both sides for "a peace
arising from a free and faithful agreement," a peace of "agreement and
concord," not the "result of a proportion of forces, but . . . a moral and
juridical process," and insists that " a real peace . . . can never be a harsh
imposition supported by arms".

And we Catholics mumble piously about our Holy Father the Pope
and go on waving the flag for Unconditional Surrender and fighting to
the last man. We shake an angry fist at every one who dares speak about
Peace Now or a Negotiated Peace.

Perhaps the fight-to-the-last-man people are right and I am the blind
one — in which case I would like some Bishop's Committee to tell me so.
If not, I would like every Catholic editor, and every Catholic clergyman,
and every other Catholic whom God gave brains enough to hold responsible to back the Pope's idea of "a peace arising from a free and fruit-
ful agreement even if it should not correspond in all points to their
aspirations."

Sincerely yours,

Austin J. App, Ph.D.

* * *

(26)

Destroying Germany and Its People

476 W. 7th Ave., Columbus 1, Ohio
May 20, 1944

Mr. Thomas Mann
1550 San Remo Drive
Pacific Palisades, California

My dear Mr. Mann:

I am unknown to you, but as a professor of literature I have followed
your work and once sent you an article of mine, which your secretary
acknowledged. What prompts me to write this particular day is that I
just happened to see your letter to Alex Tolstoi, son of the great writer,
who believed that even though there is wrong somewhere one should not
promote a war against it that will cost endless suffering, death and destruction.

You and other German refugees and millions of German Jews have
suffered particular wrong from a German regime which in some of its
particular acts was ruthless and unjust and which philosophically does
not seem as sound to us as democracy. You have been in the same position as regards Germany in which millions of Russians have been with
regards to Soviet Russia — and in which thousands of American Japanese
are with regards to our New Deal. All of you have suffered particular
and real injustice at the hands of particular governments.

If a Japanese-American escaped from Roosevelt's concentration camp,
and should in Argentina promote a world war against the United States to

crush this to him very unjust New Deal American government, the world
could understand his feelings, but he would be doing Argentina, and the
world, and the United States a great deal of harm — even though Argentina and the world would not recognize it for some years. He himself
would not realize until too late that his Argentinian war against the United
States was not finally an ideological war against one form of government
in America but a power war whose ultimate purpose and certainly effect
would be to weaken the people of the United States. And he would see
too late that his own particular grievance could not possibly justify the
immense amount of death and destruction he had been promoting (always with the best of intentions, of course).

So you, having suffered real injury at the hands of the German National Socialist government, have been promoting a world war against
that government. You may be said to have had considerable influence in
getting the belligerent acts of the destroyer deal and lend-lease bill enacted
against Germany, which had not given us any provocation whatsoever.
You pushed an ideological war, you tried to believe, against the National
Socialists. In fact you wanted to "free" Germany and to do so urged us
into a war which is costing us 300 billion dollars, perhaps a million lives
and is causing us to destroy millions of German and other European
women and children and to bomb Rome, Munich, and Berlin.

And is your ideological war to "free" Germany going to do it — and
has it increased the happiness of Poland which had been asked to give
back to Germany the very German city of Danzig the Germans had a
right to demand and ought to have demanded? Has your urging Poland
not to surrender Danzig peaceably (because though it belonged to Germany, the German government was an ideologically bad one and therefore must be treated, as I would put it, unjustly) made Poland happy?

Most of all, is this war which you urged the United States without
provocation to join against Germany turning out to be an ideological war
to "free" Europe and to "free" Germany, or is it proving to be what Lindbergh said it was, what American geopolitician Spokesman says all wars
are, just another dirty power political war?

Are you seeing that we who could not "appease" the National Socialists of Germany by letting them have what undoubtedly ought to have
been Germany's, namely Danzig, are now quite willing to appease the
Communists of Russia by giving them a large slice of Finland which is
certainly more Finnish than Danzig ever was Polish?

Are you seeing that the great promoters of the Atlantic Charter are
not only all set to "free" Germany of its Nationalist government but also
of sections of Germany which they will give to Poland as a compensation
for Communist grabs of dubious Polish territory? Are you beginning to
see that the great ideological world war you were promoting merely against
the National Socialists which had done you some particular harm is now
developing into an attempt to dismember Germany and so to ruin what
through tears and griefs and war it took Europe hundreds of years to accomplish and to set the clock back again 150 years?

Are you seeing that the great world war you promoted to free the
Germans of National Socialism is developing into destroying Germany's
industrialism and competitive power in the world markets? Are you beginning to see that justifying themselves on your testimony of Germany's
war guilt, the great ideological warmakers, in spite of protestations of no
intentions of enslaving the German people, are getting ready to impose
such reparations as will be worse than enslavement?

And do you see, as I see with shudders, and what accounts for my interest in the matter, that as we make a peace by the sword and try to keep it by the sword we will not succeed — because injustice never succeeds forever — that some decades from now I, as an American, will again have to suffer in a useless foreign war and our American boys will again have to die in Europe, and the reason will again be the phony ideological one?

I think you are beginning to see all that — too late, of course. Or largely too late. You probably belong to the Friends of Germany Committee by now — poor benighted souls who still think this is an ideological war and not dirty damnable power politics intended to crush whoever is the most efficient economic rival.

I said it is largely too late. Yes, the greatest damage has already been done. But if you and men like you would at least talk as if you saw the truth — something like a speedier and a more just peace would yet be possible. Governments want power politics; peoples want justice IF THEY SEE WHAT JUSTICE IS. If men like you help the war-crazy governments to make our people believe that it is just to execute every German official and army officer, to give sections of German territory away to Poland and Russia, to destroy Germany's heavy industry, to dismember the country, to destroy its foreign trade and economic power, to pay reparations that mean virtual enslavement — then the people will demand these atrocities as noble and just things.

But you, I hope, whose great works I have all my life admired, know that these things are atrocities, that they are the grossest injustices — and most of all, that in spite of twenty million swords hung daily over 80,000,000 people so abused, they will sooner or later find a way to rise again and slash the throats of their oppressors. Danzig was an injustice — it may have been a small one — but it did produce the incident which made it possible for men who talked like you to fan a world war.

Perhaps you can still do a little to hasten peace and to promote a little bit of justice in the peace.

But I don't think you will do it unless you come to feel as Tolstoi felt that war is bad, that to smash any nation with bombs because it has a government that is ideologically unsound is a crime, and to be specific, if it was wrong of the Germans to reclaim Danzig by force when it wasn't given them any other way, then it was just as wrong, just as much of a crime to employ force to prevent their forceful rectification of an injustice. If I owe you a thousand dollars and refuse to give it to you and the law-courts do not exist or refuse to make me give it to you and if you then finally try to wrestle it from me, any uncle of mine who would at that minute jump on you and insist on beating you up until you unconditionally surrendered would be far more wrong than you were in trying to get what really belonged to you.

We want pacifism — but not a one-sided one. Not the pacifism of those who sit on the majority of the world's goods stolen down the centuries and who want everybody else pacifistically to suffer them to have it. People who think it is a great crime for the others to shoot, but a very noble thing for them, are not pacifists. People who say that justice must be done even to the devil, that Danzig must be given to whom it belongs even if these people are at the moment not just to the Jews, and that the injustice to the Jews must be remedied by means proportioned to the harm done, not by destroying half the world — those people can be expected to do the world some good.

In the article I wrote about you some years ago I defended you as a great Christian novelist. I did this when many of my fellow Catholics were suspicious of you. I still think I was right. But politically you and those who have talked like you have made it possible for the power politicians to destroy Europe and Asia and to do this country irreparable harm, the end of which we can't see yet. I am hoping you will in what little way you still can, try to remedy some of the evil and do what you can to promote a speedy conciliatory peace.

Very truly yours,

Austin J. App, Ph.D.

(27)

War the Result of WW I Injustices

476 W. 7th Ave., Columbus 1, O.
May 29, 1944

Editor
READER'S DIGEST
Pleasantville, N. Y.

Re: Bullitt article on Versailles Tragedy

Gentlemen:

I want to express my deep satisfaction with your printing of William C. Bullitt's version of the Tragedy of Versailles.

British and American leaders have during the last four years constantly dinned into American ears that the present war is the result of a too lenient and just treatment of Germany and Austria in 1919.

The American people have caught this temper and are ready along with the leaders to perpetrate upon the world a treaty that will make the injustices of Versailles look innocent.

Already we are seeing that the Atlantic Charter principles are being abrogated in favor of territorial injustices against Germany in the interest of so-called security.

But security, as Versailles ought sufficiently to have shown, does not come from injustices. Ones very Allies may contribute, as Japan and Italy, to flaming an injustice into a world war. Security should come and can come only from justice. If it is true that a nation may go to war to correct an intolerable injustice, as we did in so many cases beginning with the Revolution, then Germany will have the right to go to war again to try to correct an injustice and so again disturb the security founded on injustices.

Germany may go to war again even if she is treated justly, but she won't have any right to. But if she is treated unjustly, and if she has as much guts as we ourselves have, she will go to war again and will have a right to — following our own precedents.

This time we must have a peace of reconciliation, of true justice — not a crooked peace dictated at the point of the sword as in 1919. A just peace offers the right to hope. An unjust peace offers no right to hope —in fact, forces right-thinking people to see it either made just—or broken! Just as death is preferable to some forms of slavery so those suffering from an unjust peace have a right to prefer war to peace or the so-called security. Security is a part of justice; it may not be a substitute for justice.

Consequently, I hope you will continue to exert your efforts towards educating the people against allowing the same criminal mistakes to happen again which ruined the world in 1919.

Sincerely yours,

Austin J. App, Ph.D.

— 29 —

Catholics Should Demand Negotiated Peace

476 W. 7th Ave., Columbus 1, O.
May 31, 1944

Mr. H. L. Binsse, Managing Editor
COMMONWEAL
386 Fourth Avenue
New York City

Dear Mr. Binsse:

It happened that on Good Friday I was able to be in New York and so called at your office. Unfortunately, though quite properly, you were closed on that day.

In addition to the friendly motive of saying hello I also wanted to see if it isn't possible to swing *Commonweal* from supporting the Unconditional Surrender Policy to supporting the Pope's policy of a peace by "agreement and concord," a peace of reconciliation and of negotiation. Not of course a peace-at-any-price, which is an absurdity, but a reasonable peace "even if it should not correspond in all points to their aspirations."

Who does not believe today that the world would be better off if Benedict's peace program of 1917 had been adopted? Who prevented its consideration? Wilson and Lansing. And at that time, did the Catholic Press, which spends so much of its space giving lipservice to the Papal pronouncements, come right out and say in a clear voice, "Yes, let's favor the Papal plan for peace (no reparations, restoration of conquered territory and of colonies, no unilateral disarmament)." Did the Catholic Press do that? No. The Catholic Press waved the flag violently and said with the right hand that the Pope is a fine fellow and with the left hand it said to Wilson and Lansing, "Make the bastards pay. Accept no negotiated peace. March to Berlin. Fight to the last man if necessary but dictate the peace so they know they are licked." That is roughly what the Catholic Press and most Catholic bishops and most Catholics in effect did in 1917-19. The Pope said and wanted one thing — but we of course knew better — we said and wanted another thing. The old damnable national prejudice which affects everybody in every country in a war — and which is wrong and has never been right.

Why do I address the *Commonweal?* Because it is always so wrong? No. Precisely because of all general Catholic (and national secular) papers it is so often right. I don't waste my time with born idiots.

In 1942 I sent you a letter about the internment of Japanese-American citizens. You returned it. But two years later you finally took the stand I presented two years earlier. I congratulate you. You were still way ahead of most papers. But why couldn't you have been absolutely right from the start? A leader must be *the* first, not the tenth or twentieth. Just think twenty years from now how it would sound if people the world over would say, "When the war-hysterical injustice against Americans of Japanese descent was committed, it was a Catholic Weekly and only a Catholic Weekly that spoke out against it — right away — while the hysteria was still on."

I was happy to note your attitude on obliteration bombing. I could hardly believe it when I noted your very advanced Christian attitude on immigration. This was splendid — it looks as if we are finally catching up with Christ.

And that is why I am appealing to you to catch up with Christ (or the Pope) in the one question which is the burning question of today — the matter of getting this murderous war finished in a reasonable peace. That is the only important matter today, and to be wrong on that is to be so badly wrong that no amount of correctness on anything else the rest of our lives can outweigh it. Being wrong in the matter of hastening a peace means the death of thousands, perhaps millions, the starvation and misery of millions, perhaps even billions, it means the impoverishments and destruction of peoples and countries so horrible as not to be imaginable. As one Pope says, who could shorten the war by one day would earn mankind's eternal gratitude.

And the Pope says, Start peace negotiations. And the Catholic Press says, "On with the war. Give us Unconditional Surrender and a dictated peace and make it hard this time." And let no one quibble that the Catholic Press insists on a just peace — so does Stalin. So does Churchill. when he says that for security reasons Germany must give some very German territory up to Poland to compensate Poland for Russia's *security* adjustments. People who don't agree with the Pope's method for getting peace don't want a just peace. People who are afraid to present their precise terms, don't want a just peace — they want to enforce crooked and indecent terms. And I am sure, down in your heart, you know it.

Would you if you were a German accept Unconditional Surrender while one bullet was left to fire? Would you or I as Americans give up to any one invading us from Europe who demanded Unconditional Surrender while we had a bullet left to shoot? Let's not expect of other human beings what we would not consider decent ourselves.

And let no one say that Unconditional Surrender isn't meant that way. If it isn't, then let's say that it isn't and not try to humiliate any nation unnecessarily. The Pope speaks out precisely in favor of saving an enemy's face. Why must we be dishonest and hypocritical?

Also, I am convinced that men who on so many things see so clearly, much more clearly than most editors, know that the Pope favors a negotiated peace, one of reconciliation, one in which no side is completely crushed, one which is a compromise, not a harsh dictation. I am convinced you know this — only one who doesn't ever think or whom God has punished with a special dose of nationalistic blindness can fail to see it.

Why therefore do you not come out in favor of a negotiated peace? Perhaps popular prejudice has already been so maddened by the Unconditional Surrenderists that you fear its animosity. I can understand that. I, too, cannot say everything I ought to say. But I believe you need not be unduly afraid if you start presenting the Papal view in letters such as mine of March 16, which I hereby again beg you to print. (THE PRESENT LETTER is of course to you personally and not for publication.) I must close. I know you are busy — but this matter is the most important in your and in my life. Even should we disagree violently on this we will often in the future have to be on the same platform — consequently I beg you to take time to let me know your views.

Austin J. App

Danzig and The Right of Self-Determination

476 W. 7th Ave., Columbus 1, O.
July 20, 1944

Mr. Alexander Gardiner, Editor
455 West 22nd Street
Chicago, Ill.

Dear Mr. Gardiner:

Paul Gallico in his Father and Son article, which you praise, says, "The entire generation of German youth is as poisonous and dangerous as a puff adder."

Ernie Pyle in HERE IS YOUR WAR, p. 279, says regarding German prisoners in Tunisia, "The first contacts of our troops with prisoners were extremely pleasant! So pleasant in fact that American officers got to worrying because the men found the Germans so likeable."

In short, from all reports I have read written by accredited and responsible writers, the German soldier today is as fine and decent an individual as the American soldier is. The old Legionnaires in the last war, when occupying Germany, made the same discovery. They found that the German people were more decent and civilized than the peoples of their Allies. You remember that.

The truth is we are fighting the Germans only because they are so decent and civilized. Decency makes for strength and the Germans are stronger than any nation in the world except us Americans. And we don't like rivals — so we fight them. And that is why the British, our "kith and kin" as Churchill is fond of saying, fight them.

You say the Germans started five wars since 1866. Did you ever count up how many we started? The 1914 war was started when the Austria-Hungarians attacked Serbia after a murder. Germany simply helped Austria after Russia mixed its fist into what was none of her business. In 1920 the Poles attacked Lithuania to take the city of Wilno. It didn't end in a world war because Britain did not jump to the aid of Lithuania. When Germany in 1939, after waiting 20 years, finally decided to use force to get back the completely German city of Danzig, an incident of a few days, it became a world war because Britain, abetted by Roosevelt, decided to support the unjust sequestration of Danzig from Germany. The question is not whether the Germans finally used force to get Danzig, but whether Danzig was a German city or not. Would we sit idly by forever if a Versailles Treaty had given Houston to Mexico? Answer that honestly, absolutely honestly — and your idea of this war will become worthy of an intelligent man and an editor who influences millions of people. We must not expect the Germans to stand for injustice any more willingly than we would stand for it.

In 1860 we attacked Southern states because they wanted to exercise their right of self-determination. In 1876 we attacked and massacred a lot of Sioux Indians. It did not develop into a World War because Germany had the decency to keep its nose out. In 1898 we attacked and highway robbed Spain. It did not become a World War because Germany, etc., had the decency to keep their nose out. In 1899 we began the Philippine-American War, a very atrocious one. It did not become a world war because Germany had the decency and sense to keep its nose out. In 1900 we crashed into China with our Marines in the Boxer insurrection. It did not become a world war because Japan and Germany did not rush

to the aid of the Chinese and tell us to get the hell out, as we told the
Japanese on November 26, 1941. In 1914 at Vera Cruz we made an attack
upon Mexico for nothing more than a flag misdemeanor. If the Germans
had now rushed to the aid of Mexico, as we encouraged Britain to rush
to the aid of Poland in 1939, it would have been a world war — and we
would have started it — by your logic. In 1916 we again commenced an
assault upon Mexico to punish Villa (the way Austria in 1914 had entered
Serbia to punish the murderers of its crownprince). Luckily for us, Mexico was as weak as Poland and no Germany or France or Italy or Japan
stuck its nose and fists into the affair. In 1917 we got into a war that
was none of our business in order to tell Europeans what kind of government they should have — to make the world free for democracy. In 1927
we invaded Nicaragua and beat hell out of them and luckily, because Germany had the decency not to stick its nose in and help Nicaragua, a world
war was averted — but not through any virtue of our own. In 1941 when
Germany had not done us any harm in the least, we gave her enemy fifty
reconditioned destroyers while hypocritically protesting our neutrality,
we repaired British war ships in our ports; and finally under the lendlease
bill we bombed both German and Japanese troops with our lendleased
bombers, operated by Americans—before Pearl Harbor, while we were
committing one act of war after another, neither nation had done anything
whatever to us.

I repeat, the only reason we are at war with Germany is that we don't
like anybody in Europe so civilized and so efficient that our kith and kin,
Britain, can't kick them around and tell them what they may or may not
do. There is nothing ethical whatever involved — except that we have no
business mixing with our *fists* in European quarrels. And the only reason
we are fighting Japan is that there too we don't want any nation so well
organized, therefore so civilized (though still below our level) as to chal-
lenge our kith and kin's hundred-year-old prerogative of telling the Asia-
tics what they may or may not do. There is nothing ethical about it—
except that it is a crime for us to use our immense strength to interfere
with the logical development in other continents when we would not for a
moment tolerate either Japan's or Germany's interference in Mexico or
Nicaragua.

This is a long letter. It has taken effort to write it. I did not write
it for fun. I believe you to be important enough and honest enough to
merit this effort. You influence millions of Legionnaires, of whom I am one.

We lost the peace in 1919 because of ideas Gallico and you expressed
in the July issue. Instead of insisting on Wilson's just Fourteen Points,
we finally made the impossible and vengeful Peace of Versailles. If the
Germans had forever accepted that peace they would have been the demons
Gallico makes them, the kind of people who never could have fathered Eisenhower, Nimitz, Spaatz, Krueger, or Wilkie. This time we have got to be
just. The Germans have the same right and *duty* to a united and complete Germany as we have to a complete and united U.S.. We must
help them to it — or expect them to try to unite again. They must try
to unite — it is their duty — it is the thing Lincoln fought both the South
and Britain to accomplish. We Balkanized and mutilated them in 1919
— we must not do it again this time. Men like you must help preserve
an historical perspective and common sense.

Sincerely yours,

Austin J. App, Ph.D.

Stalin Surely not Peace-Loving

476 W. 7th Ave., Columbus 1, O.
August 3, 1944

Mr. Alexander Gardiner, Editor
American Legion Magazine
One Park Avenue, New York

Dear Mr. Gardiner:

Because it requires more human discipline than most people have to answer a letter which disagrees with one's views and not to throw it angrily away, I want to express to you my appreciation for your straightforward and detailed answer.

I also sympathized with your wrath at my not including the Japanese and Germans in our Chinese Boxer exploit. Of course, I knew we were all foraging in China together at the time. I meant to suggest, however, that among governments there is no ethics except that I *and* we are right and *you* are wrong, that is, the other fellow. When we were all plaguing China together then Germany and Japan too were quite noble and "peace-loving." Haven't you sometimes smiled the way Mr. Roosevelt speaks of the grand "peace-loving" Big Four forever hence forward on holding the bayonett over the wicked aggressors Germany, Japan, and Italy to teach them the ways of peace — when one of the great peace lovers attacked Finland in 1939 and swallowed up three other independent nations and when two of the big wicked and incurable peacedisturbers were our beloved peaceloving allies only twenty years ago? Hasn't that word "peace-loving" so applied made you realize that among governments the ethics to be fair to the other side does not exist — but the only ethics governments know is that I and my side are right and the other side is Satanic.

BUT teachers, and writers, and editors MUST not let their governments get away with such unfairness. We must insist on honesty and justice to friends and foes alike.

I also meant to suggest that whether we eventually call a nation "peace-loving" or wicked depends a great deal on what we do or did in the first place. I maintain for example that if Mr. Roosevelt had violated the constitution and our neutrality by giving Germany fifty reconditioned destroyers instead, as he did, giving them to Britain, then we would today be calling Germany "peace-loving" and England a wicked aggressor, a monarchistic tyranny, a vile oppressor of 350,000,000 peoples in Asia whom we must "liberate!"

In other words, wars are despicable power politics — and moral slogans are only used to trick clergymen and professors and editors into sanctioning wholesale slaughter.

But what I really beg of you is with regard to the matter of a "soft" or "harsh" peace. Please, in your capacity as editor recognize those words as simply hypocrisy for a "just" or an "unjust" peace. The "harsh" peace people want an unjust peace as at Versailles. And believe me, they will get what they got then — slaughter and misery and bloodshed a few decades later. If Danzig is German, justice requires it be given her — and there simply aren't two ways about it. It was wrong for the Germans to use force to achieve the just return of Danzig, but it was *still more wrong,* note this heavily, for Poland and Britain and us to use force to prevent the doing of this justice.

While peace is desirable always — I favor a negotiated peace now —

yet peace must not be expected until reasonable justice is done. If we treat the Germans unjustly, if we don't grant them the unity we granted the Britains and the French and the Italians, and fought a Civil War to keep for ourselves, then we must expect the Germans to fight and to fight again, and still again, until they are all dead, or until they have achieved what justice and Christianity require.

To say we and Britain and Russia will keep using our bayonetts to prevent this just union of Germany is to advocate an indefensible injustice. To say that we will succeed that way to preserve the peace of Europe is to suppose that God will permanently sanction and favor our gross injustice. He did not do it in 1919. I tell you history indicates that He will not do it in 1944.

I beg you as an editor not to use the words harsh or soft peace, but to keep talking of a just and unjust peace. Don't let our boys down again as we did in 1919. We must have justice. AND JUSTICE MEANS NOT TO DO TO THE GERMANS AND THE JAPANESE WHAT, IF THEY WON, WE WOULD CONSIDER WRONG IF THEY DID TO US.

I realize you are in the majority with about 135 millions of Americans just now. But remember in every war the majority has proven itself wrong and put on sack cloth and ashes ten years afterwards. In 1847 Lincoln was called a traitor and lost his seat in Congress; in Germany during the Napoleonic war Goethe was considered un-German and treasonable, in 1917 LaFollette was considered unpatriotic, ten years later they erected a statue to him in Washington!

You have been kind enough to answer me once. I would not have written this second letter if I believed that it would put you to the trouble of answering me again. This is more to thank you than anything else. But someday perhaps we can meet over a cocktail — for if the peace proves as unjust as it now appears to be in the making you will hear of me often — and someday I am sure you will come pretty close to agreeing with me. Between 1919 and 1939 I saw the criminal injustice and let it ride; this time I'll do my bit to correct it before another Hitler rises to try to do it.

Sincerely yours,

Austin J. App

(31)

Wilson's Fourteen Points Violated

476 W. 7th Ave., Columbus, O.
August 7, 1944

LIFE MAGAZINE
Rockefeller Center
New York 20

To the Editor:

Belatedly I get a chance to endorse William Ernest Hocking's article, "America's World Purpose", in the April 17 issue.

Few things are more timely than Dr. Hocking's reminder that we are in World War II, not because the 1919 peace was too soft, but because our Allies insisted on making it too unjust. He is right to remind us that our Allies discarded nine of Wilson's just Fourteen Points, so that we could hardly be expected to approve the Versailles Treaty.

I add that an honorable nation has no right to underwrite an unjust Treaty. This time America has to insist that the treaty is just. If our

Allies insist on making another unjust treaty, such as robbing Germany of East Prussia in order to balance Russia's robbery of half of Poland, then we must again withdraw our support. America certainly cannot use its bayonetts to help robbers keep their unjust loot!

Before it is too late, therefore, let's heed the implications of Bullitt's picture of the Tragedy of Versailles and demand that our Administration, which used the Atlantic Charter to edge us into the war, now make it the condition of any lend-lease or any other help. If the Allies want their kind of peace, then let them fight their own war — and let's have no nonsense about it. We want no "soft" peace or "harsh" peace — what we want this time is a *just* peace — and that means among other things, no territorial robberies.

Sincerely yours,

Austin J. App, Ph.D.

(32)

East Prussia Likened to Texas

476 W. 7th Ave., Columbus 1, O.
August 7, 1944

The Columbus DISPATCH
Columbus, Ohio

To the Editor:

Ever since Moscow declared that for taking a half of Poland, Russia intends to recompense Poland by giving her a part of Germany, London and Washington are exerting a lot of propaganda pressure to make the American people tolerate this crooked horsedeal.

At first everybody was horrified at the preposterous suggestion of robbing Germany of its ancient province of East Prussia. We remembered that Churchill and Roosevelt in the Atlantic Charter, with which they slid us into the war, distinctly promised no territorial robberies. In fact they implied that America had to get into the war so there would be a just peace without such territorial robberies.

But, now, because Stalin wants to swallow three whole countries, and rob Finland and Poland of large territories, London and Washington suddenly think they can pay Poland by cutting whole provinces off Germany.

The thing for us Americans to remember is that East Prussia is as German as Texas is American. No red-blooded American would ever tolerate anybody's robbing us of Texas. Sooner or later we would fight for it even if we had to do it with pitchforks.

The second thing to remember is that we would not stand for the Germans won't stand for. They are exactly the kind of people we are, so much so that fellows like Eisenhower, Nimitz, Spaatz, and Krueger are of German descent. East Prussia is the Texas of Germany. There is nothing more German in Germany than the East Prussians. To hand East Prussia to any other nation is a criminal injustice. It is something no German will or ought to tolerate. But more than that, it is something no American must tolerate. If we are fighting for anything, it is for justice everywhere in the world.

We let London and Paris ruin Wilson's Fourteen Points in 1919 so that they made a peace which no decent American could endorse. We

— 36 —

must not this time again let somebody else ruin the Atlantic Charter and make a peace which no self-respecting American can support.

Cutting East Prussia away from Germany is as great a crime as cutting Texas from the United States would be. Every one of us should try to influence Congress and the Administration to keep Washington from perpetrating this Stalin-inspired peace monstrocity.

Austin J. App, Ph.D.

------◆●◆------

(33)

A Harsh Peace is an Unjust Peace

476 W. 7th Ave., Columbus 1, O.
August 8, 1944

Mr. William Shirer
Care of American Legion Magazine
455 West 22nd Street, Chicago, Ill.

My dear Mr. Shirer:

I am writing you in reference to your article "Soft Peace — World War III" in the August American Legion Magazine. Long ago I read with admiration your Berlin Diary. I admired it especially because it set the tone for reasonable decency and honesty in describing the other side in a war. The filthy and lying atrocity mongering of the last war has therefore been absent in most respectable journalists and confined to people like Walter Winchell, and mystery thriller writers.

In this particular article you bring out a truth that unfortunately you should have emphasized before Roosevelt succeeded in destroyer-dealing and lend-leasing us into the war. It is that Nazism is not what we are fighting about and is not the root of the German problem. You are right in saying that, and Lindbergh was therefore also right in saying that shouting that Nazism must be wiped off the earth was simply Rooseveltian propaganda to get us into the war.

As Voigt, the editor of *Nineteenth Century and After* says, England would rather have a weak totalitarian Germany than a strong democratic Germany. In other words this is the old power politics war in which Britain refuses to let anyone in Europe be stronger than herself. Since in fact however Germany is stronger than she, and nothing but mass murder of thirty million Germans can prevent it, she has to play up the "kith and kin" stuff to get us into every one of her power political wars to make her European "boss" again.

You are right in saying the German people are behind Hitler's efforts to get Danzig back. The question is, shouldn't they be? Would we tolerate anybody's having given Galveston to Mexico? The Germans waited twenty years to get that robbery back peacefully. Wasn't that long enough to wait, or at any rate, would we in like circumstances have waited longer? That is important, Would we in like circumstances have waited longer?

The German Problem is that England, France, Spain, Russia, even Italy was allowed to unite without gross interference from outsiders but the 245 German states have not been allowed to unite without England and France making war upon them whenever that union was progressing. Under Hitler that union, long overdue, was almost complete except for Danzig and that monstrous corridor (which no nation would have tolerated, certainly not we). Unfortunately just when this long over-due (and eventually absolutely certain and necessary) union was about fin-

— 37 —

ished, England and France again determined Poland not to give up the wrongly possessed parts and rather plunged the world into a war than permit the just union of Germany.

There you have a much more honest and true picture of Europe's troubles the last 200 years, even if somewhat oversimplified, than implied in the insanity of every twenty-five years denouncing some German government as the beast of Berlin with which no one can negotiate peace, or do business.

The German Problem will be solved when Prussia, Austria, Bavaria, Saxony, etc., and Danzig, and of course East Prussia and the Rhineland are under one flag, where they belong and where they someday will be. We fought a civil war to keep the North and South of the United States together. The Germans would be spineless ninnies if they would not try and try again to do what every people in the world has done or must try to do — form into a great and greater brotherhood. The fact that in the German case such a union would make Germany stronger than Great Britain gives neither Britain nor us nor anybody else the right to prevent it. To try to prevent it by bombs and murder is criminal.

If we don't make a just peace this time, one which solves the German problem in the only correct way, union of all those who want to belong to a German central European state, and granting such influence over close neighboring states as Bohemia as we are willing to let Russia have over Latvia, and as we claim over Cuba, then there will be a third world war — and there should be one. It would be the world's worst crime if an injustice should be permanently frozen by a world police force. Only such a peace should be preserved which is a just peace. A just peace is one, which if circumstances were reversed, *we* would be willing to accept.

You say the Germans depend on our forgiving and forgetting. Let me ask what have we Americans to forgive and forget. What did the Germans do to us? I remember that when we were neutral we gave her enemy fifty warships, we also repaired her enemy's battleships in our neutral ports, we lendleased billions of planes and things to her enemy (while we were professedly neutral). That is what we did to Germany. I don't remember anything they did to us. Frankly, what did they do to us before we gave her enemy fifty destroyers? It seems to me the problem is to get the *Germans* to forgive and to forget. That is the big problem. It is up to us to convince them that in the future we will treat all European nations and governments impartially — that we will treat the attacker of Poland exactly and no different than the attacker of Finland, that we will treat a National Socialistic government exactly as we have treated a Communistic or monarchistic one. That is our problem — to convince the Germans of that — and so to persuade them to forgive and to forget.

Honestly now, aside from the usual war propagandistic dishonesty which makes Hull claim we are fighting Naziism, isn't that the truth now and the problem. The word soft peace is another word for just peace, and harsh peace is the word for an unjust peace. Do you as an American insist on an unjust peace, and do you reject a just peace? I can't believe it. Consequently I hope you will not again use those hypocritical words. If you mean an unjust peace, at least say so. That isn't too much to ask of us Americans, it seems to me.

Sincerely yours,

Austin J. App, Ph.D.

East Prussia and the Atlantic Charter

476 W. 7th Ave.,
Columbus 1, Ohio
August 18, 1944

AMERICA
329 West 108th Street
New York City, N. Y.

To the Editor:

When the lease-lend bill and the destroyer-deal were being promulgated, American statesmen and commentators filled the air with such Christian statements regarding a just peace as are typified in the Atlantic Charter. All territorial robberies were vetoed.

But ever since what Mr. Churchill said he dreamed of, aimed at, and worked for was effected, our full participation in the war, the former statements envisioning a JUST peace have changed to assurances of an ENFORCED peace.

However, it is extremely important to remember, ENFORCING a peace is not the problem at all. Surely a victorious Germany could have ENFORCED a peace as well as a victorious Russia. The real Christian problem is to make a JUST peace. If the peace is UNJUST then it is a crime to enforce it. It is obviously wrong to enforce an injustice. Nor is there a "soft" or "harsh" peace; there is only a just or an unjust peace.

One of the injustices now being trial-ballooned upon the American people, under initial Russian inspiration, is robbing Germany of East Prussia. But East Prussia has been German since the thirteenth century, several hundred years before the Americans took America from the Indians.

If East Prussia, in violation of the Atlantic Charter, is torn from Germany, the peace would be an unjust one. In such an event decent Americans could no more ethically enforce it than they found it ethical to enforce the equally unjust Versailles peace.

Sincerely

Austin J. App, Ph.D.

German Right to Full Unity

Fall, 1944

To the *San Antonio Light*:

Recently on his 88th birthday when Bernard Shaw was asked how to keep the Germans from jumping at Europe's throat, he answered, "Treat them decently and they won't jump at anybody's throat."

Until England did justice to Ireland, the Irish were the most rebellious people in the world. Until England and France let the Germans do what every other people has been allowed to do there will be a German problem. All the Germans of central Europe who want to belong to one Reich must be allowed to belong to one Reich—the Sudetens, and the Danzigers, and the Austrians, just like the Rhinelanders, and the Bavarians, and the Prussians. Every important war in Europe since the Thirty years war 300 years ago was essentially due to the fact that France or England or both by bribery and force tried to keep the Germans Balkanized. If we treat them justly then like the Irish they will be satisfied—until then they shouldn't be satisfied.

Austin J. App, Ph.D.
146 Davis Court
San Antonio, Texas

———◄•►———

(36)

Morgenthau's Genocidic Plan for Germans
Compared with Spencer's for the Irish

146 Davis Court, San Antonio, Texas
October 11, 1944

Mr. Henry Morganthau, Jr.
Secretary of the Treasury
Washington, D. C.

My dear Mr. Morgenthau:

For the last several weeks I have been in a state of exaltation because of the perception that, just as in the military phase it was precisely we Americans who achieved the bombing of Rome, so in the political phase of the war it would be precisely an American who in the long pages of history had succeeded in making the most atrocious and barbarous proposal for the treatment of a vanquished nation.

I was of course thinking of your notorious plan for destroying and keeping destroyed all the factories and shops of Germany so that eighty million people could slowly die of undernourishment without our having to waste poison gas or bullets to kill them off individually. It seemed to me particularly felicitous that the author of this proposal should be an American of the Jewish persuasion, which has always been accused of holding and practicing the barbarism expressed in the words, "eye for an eye and tooth for a tooth."

But today I am momentarily de-exalted. Today I unexpectedly remembered the plan of the British poet Edmund Spenser for "pacifying the oppressed and rebellious people" of Ireland. He proposed that England send a huge force of cavalry and infantry into Ireland and to hunt the Irish down "like wild beasts." He calculated further that cold, exposure, famine and sickness, after two winters of hunting them down, could be trusted to exterminate the remnant of this "oppressed and rebellious people." After that, he argued, he believed the country would be peaceful.

Now, I submit, regretfully, that the poet Spenser's plan exceeds in imaginative cruelty and atrociousness your plan for the extermination of the Germans; I don't think you should let him "get away with that." In as much as you have made such a good start in surpassing and exceeding nearly the whole record of barbarous peace proposals I suggest that you try again and see whether you cannot offer a proposal still more barbarous and bloodthirsty and revengeful, one which in that respect could nose out Edmund Spenser's, so that you might become the undisputed titleholder of the world's most atrocious peace plan and so that through you, all of us Americans might share in that honor vicariously, as we shared in the bombing of Rome.

Very sincerely yours,

Austin J. App, Ph.D.

— 40 —

Sudetenland, Danzig, Memel and German Unity

146 Davis Court, San Antonio, Texas
October 12, 1944

COMMONWEAL
386—4th Avenue
New York City

To the Editor:

I was happy to see that you do not endorse Mr. Morgenthau's heavy-weight bit of barbarism, the Balkanization and de-industrialization of Germany. (And then they say this war is fought against national socialism, and not to rid the world of a commercial competitor.)

Parenthetically—there is no soft or harsh peace: there is only a just or unjust peace, as all of us still knew when the Atlantic Charter was promulgated as a tool for "idealizing" us into the war!

Specifically I want to make only one simple point. There will be no peace in central Europe (and if we believe that injustice must not become permanent, there should be no peace in central Europe) until the people there are allowed to do what the English people, and the French people, and the Italian people have long ago been allowed to do. All the contiguous people of central Europe who, (because they are just like the French and the British and like us Americans), want to belong to one Reich must be encouraged and permitted to do so.

All honest observers know that, according to the fair evidence of the last twenty years, the people who want to be under one flag are: Prussia (and East Prussia), Bavaria, Saxony, the Rhineland, Wuerttemberg, Silesia, Schleswig-Holstein, AUSTRIA, the SUDETENLAND, MEMEL, and DANZIG.

Since the Thirty years war, in which France succeeded in getting the Protestant Germans (Prussians) to split from the Catholic Germans, that crime of keeping the brothers apart by force or by bribery has been the cancer of Europe.

Someday they will be allowed to live as one family, just as one day Ireland was allowed to be free. AND DANZIG WILL BE WITH THE REST. Britain, with the criminal and stupid help of the United States, may prevent this elemental, homogenous fraternizing of the Germans, demanded by progress and Christianity, for another dozen world wars. But God won't let even the United States succeed forever in imposing a major crime upon the world. And someday all these central Europeans will be allowed to be together. And then the German "problem" will have ended. Until then it will not end—AND SHOULD NOT END. Justice is above peace.

If one must strip the war to its essential and indicate a just peace in its minimum essentials—there it is.

Sincerely,

Austin J. App

(38)

Clare Booth Luce on Roosevelt's Lying

146 Davis Court, San Antonio, Texas
October 15, 1944

(*Copy to Mr. Thomas E. Dewey, Presidential Candidate*)

The Columbus Dispatch
Columbus, Ohio
To the Editor:

Clare Booth Luce, in her Friday night speech, finally rolled up against Mr. Roosevelt a slogan which is both powerful and honest. He "lied us into a war because he did not have the political courage to lead us into it."

This is the slogan that can, and it is the slogan that should, bounce Mr. Roosevelt out of the presidency. It is the one that SHOULD because it is the most important and the truest charge that can be made against the President of the American people which is now killing a thousand American boys a day.

Mrs. Luce could have added, and I hope she soon will, that Mr. Roosevelt not only "lied us into a war," but has also already begun losing the peace for us—in Finland, in Poland, in the Baltic Republics, in Rumania, in Jugoslavia. It ought to be shouted from every platform and corner: He lied us into the war and he's losing the peace—and we're through with him and all his Rooseveltians.

Sincerely,

Austin J. App, Ph.D.

*   *   *

Dear Mr. Dewey:

I thing lying us into the war and losing the peace are the most powerful and honest and important issues against the Roosevelt Administration. I believe if you were to start hitting that and hitting it hard again and again you would win easily and HONORABLY.

Sincerely,

A. J. App

---

(39)

The Word "Hun" and American Generals
like Eisenhower

146 Davis Court, San Antonio, Texas
November 1, 1944

Knickerbocker Weekly
30 Rockefeller Plaza,
New York 20, N. Y.
Gentlemen:

Because like most other Americans I am extremely sorry for the tragedy that the great powers of the world inflicted on such good and small nations as Holland, Belgium, Finland, Latvia, Lithuania, Norway, Iceland, and Greece, I make it a point as often as possible to read your magazine devoted to arousing sympathy for the Netherlands. When honestly and fairly done, there can hardly be a nobler purpose than that of your magazine.

Because I don't want to see such a good motive and purpose vitiated in any way I permit myself two slight criticisms.

— 42 —

I note you regularly apply the word "Hun" to the Germans. Now "Hun" is a generic word, just like the word Teuton. If, for example, the Dutch are Teutons, then they remain Teutons even should they emigrate to a different country. A dog, for example, a German police dog, remains a dog even after he comes to America, and all his grandchildren remain dogs. If, as you say, the Germans are "Huns," then people of German descent in this country are "Huns." That means that General Eisenhower is a "Hun," by your use of the word, and Spaatz, Nimitz, Krueger, the late Wilkie all are "Huns."

I don't like to believe that they are, and I wonder whether you would mind not to use that word anymore. I notice Mr. Churchill uses it too, in your way, but then Mr. Churchill also believes in keeping 350,000,000 Indians enslaved, and therefore we can't justify a slanderous usage by him.

You speak very praisingly and eloquently of the many Dutchmen who under the German occupation engaged in underground activities—sabotage, insurrectionist newspapers, etc. As you know, General Eisenhower has told the people of Germany that these things are against international law and when during American occupation any German man, woman, or child is so caught, the penalty is death. And not only for sabotage and insurrectionist printings, but even for any false information given to American authorities. If now any German guilty of such acts is executed, we and you will insist that this is not murder on our part but internationally legal execution.

Now I notice you speak of "Twenty-three Patriots Murdered" by the Germans for underground activities as those above, which you also speak about elsewhere in the magazine. It seems to me one cannot have it both ways. If you and we want Dutchmen to engage in internationally outlawed activities under German occupation, then we have to accept German execution of those so caught. Isn't that right? And any German execution of Dutch saboteurs is no more or less murder than General Eisenhower's execution of German saboteurs. I think that honesty and fairness are always good policy, even in war.

Sincerely yours,

Austin J. App, Ph.D.

━━━━━━━◀●▶━━━━━━━

(40)

Atlantic Charter Applies to Germany as Much as to Poland

146 Davis Court, San Antonio 2, Texas
November 5, 1944

Rt. Rev. Michael J. Ready, General Secretary,
    National Catholic Welfare Council
1312 Massachusetts Ave., N. W.
Washington, D. C.

Dear Msgr. Ready:

You will probably be surprised to get a letter from me complimenting you upon your October 23 speech in Toledo. As you, or at least some of your colleagues know, I have been consistently horrified and angered at the NCWC's war-blind policy of urging the killing of Italians because there were fascists and sinners and the killing of Germans because they are national socialists and sinners. To me this policy seems to actualize

what critics have always alleged against the Inquisition, namely, that
Catholics have thought it a right and even a holy crusading duty to kill
those human beings whose belief differs from theirs. Father John A.
Ryan, for example, urging our boys to kill bravely says, "What ideal
could be higher, or more worthwhile, than that of ridding the world of
pagan Nazism?" In other words, the NCWC might anytime extend its
ideal to killing the pagan Communists, or the pagan Mohammedans, or
the pagan wretches of British-occupied India, etc., etc.

But, though I am in horrified opposition to the above policy of yours,
as I gathered it from many quotations, I am happy to endorse your recent
plea that the first point of the Atlantic Charter, as between Poland and
Russia, must be observed. I was however more particularly pleased at
your saying,

> *The problem of Poland is not whether it will receive from
> Germany territory equal in extent to that which Russia
> takes from it in the East . . .*

There you began to touch the real principle for which we Catholics
must stand. Christ kept warning us that even the pagans fight for justice
to their friends and relatives, but that a Christian is known for fighting
for justice for everybody, even particularly for his enemies.

Now, if we Catholics only seem to remember the Atlantic Charter
point about no territorial transferences without consent of the people
with regard to Catholic Poland, more or less because Poland is Catholic,
and acquiesce in the violation of that point with regard to enemy or Protestant countries, we cannot fail to earn and to deserve the contempt of
the world — for then we are even as the pagans of whom Jesus speaks
again and again.

Whether we Catholics love justice for justice sake or merely for re-
ligious-partisan-political sake will evidence itself more than in anything
else in our insistence or non-insistence on the just application of the Atlantic Charter to our so-called "enemies."

Mindful of Point One of the Atlantic Charter, will the NCWC insist
as strongly, for example, that East Prussia be not transferred without
the consent of its people as it will insist that no part of Poland will be
transferred to Russia without the consent of its people? That is the
touchstone as to whether we are true lovers of justice, or merely political-
religious power politicians.

When you insist that the first point of the Atlantic Charter be observed, do you realize, for example, and do you mean it to be honored, that
the people of Danzig and of Memel and of Silesia and of Austria and of
the Sudeten Land absolutely must not be torn from anybody without their
majority consent and absolutely must be allowed to cast in their lot with
whom their majority (fairly decided of course) wish?

If you do that, then you really love justice for justice sake. And
then you must speak out to that effect and so must the whole NCWC.

And if all of us Catholics do that and if we succeed in making the
countries honor the Atlantic Charter in this full sense, as it applies to
friends, neutrals, and "enemies", then we will have peace that is a just
peace, and such a just peace is the only kind of peace a real Catholic will
have the right to try to enforce. A Catholic must try to alter any unjust
peace; only a gangster may enforce an unjust peace. Already no Catholic
may help Russia enforce its peace against Finland. And if the Danzigers
are not allowed to stay where they wish, or go where they wish, if terri-

torially and contiguously possible, then should they someday rebel, only a scoundrel will bomb them to pieces for insisting on Point One of the Atlantic Charter.

I keep repeating Danzig because that brings the problem down to earth, for I hate hypocritical and glittering generalities.

You can imagine, therefore, that I was happy to detect in your above quoted sentence a suggestion that your interpretation of the Atlantic Charter will not tolerate robbing "enemy" Peter in order to pay "friend" Paul. I hope, I do hope and pray, I am right and that you and your NCWC colleagues, men whose ability I have always respected and some of whom, like Father John A Ryan, have shaped my whole life and thinking, will stress that Atlantic Charter more and more clearly and effectively all the time.

Very sincerely yours,

Austin J. App, Ph.D.

---

(41)

Catholics, National Socialists, Communists — Ideological Wars

146 Davis Court, San Antonio 2, Texas
November 5, 1944

THE CHRISTIAN CENTURY
440 South Dearborn Street
Chicago, Illinois

To the Editor:

In April I attended the meetings of the Catholic Association for International Peace, virtually an arm of the National Catholic Welfare Conference, and in July at Antioch College the Institute for International Relations, under the auspices of the Friends. As a Catholic layman and college teacher, I seemed to detect a radically different approach towards justifying this war. And I wonder whether any such difference does prevail between Protestantism generally and Catholicism.

At the Antioch Institute, our part in the war seemed to be justified, if at all, solely as a self-defence measure in the sense that if we do not kill the Germans they will kill us, kill us physically.

But the dominant Catholic justification of this war, as expressed by the National Catholic Welfare Conference and several leading members of the hierarchy, is that since national socialism is a political philosophy repugnant to Catholic political philosophy we must kill Germans until they give up national socialism.

The Right Reverend John A. Ryan, director of the department of Social Action, NCWC, outstanding Catholic spokesman, answering a soldier who "expressed a wish for some higher ideal to battle for, in addition to that of national patriotism," wrote pointedly, "What ideal could be higher or more worthwhile, than that of ridding the world of pagan Nazism?" Msgr. Ryan continues that in this destruction of pagan Nazism, our soldiers "today have an ideal that they could regard as well worth fighting for and dying for" (*The Catholic Universe Bulletin*, "Totalitarianism — New and Ugly," December 18, 1942, p. 88).

As if emphasizing that the chief justification of our war lies in destroying national socialism (and therefore in killing national socialists) Archbishop Spellman has addressed our soldiers about to kill Italian fascists and German national socialists as "modern crusaders," and regularly uses words suggestive of holy crusading.

Furthermore, nearly all American Catholic spokesmen are constantly embarrassed and apologetic of the fact, as Mr. Burnet Hershey (*Liberty*, September 9, 1944) expresses it, that "The Pope has said nothing about the destruction of Nazism." They answer apologetically, in the words of Professor F. A. Herman, "However, the demand for the destruction of Nazism is implied in everything ever said by any competent Catholic writer about natural law and natural rights" (*Our Sunday Visitor*, October 22, 1944).

In other words, while the Pope has said nothing to show that he thinks Germans must be killed until they give up national socialism and that no peace can or may be negotiated with any national socialistic government (with which he once negotiated a Concordat), the dominant American Catholic spokesmen hold that killing Germans because they are national socialists is the one greatest aim and justification of the war, as seen in Father Ryan's words.

Since the *Christian Century* is a representative Protestant publication, I would appreciate some expression as to whether this Catholic attitude meets with its endorsement or whether it raises some doubts and apprehensions in the minds of the *Christian Century* editors.

Specifically I am wondering whether the *Christian Century* sees any analogy between the present Catholic injunction to kill Germans for their national socialism* with the Seventeenth Century practice in the Thirty Years War in which Catholics killed Germans who remained "heretically" Lutheran, and Lutherans killed Austrians and Bavarians who remained stubbornly Catholic.

Furthermore, would the *Christian Century* consider it a logical development if men like Father John A. Ryan, who now urge the killing of Germans because they hold the un-Catholic philosophy of national socialism, should eventually extend their program to killing Russians because they hold the even more un-Catholic philosophy of Communism?

We laymen, both Catholic and Protestant, have I think a right to a little help in these matters from spokesmen of all persuasions, and for that reason I humbly beg of you just a brief comment on my query.

Respectfully yours,

Austin J. App, Ph.D.

Editorial note added Nov. 28, 1965:

Several explanations are needed here. First, curiously enough, the very elements whose main ostensible motive for killing Germans was to destroy their national socialism quite hypocritically allied themselves with the infinitely more godless Communism of Soviet Russia and even now keep urging appeasement.

Secondly, this was not so much a Catholic or Protestant heresy as a Rooseveltian, Jewish, and secular one. But the pity is that Christian leaders did not effectively protest against it as fatal to a good peace, for if Americans could kill Germans until they became our type democrats then the Soviets could kill them until they became their type "democrats," and that is what they did in the Soviet zone—and, quite logically, also in all the satellites. The morality of the matter is that America has no right to force peoples to give up their form of government if the people want it. It had a right to kill Germans only as long as they refused to give up territory whose people did not want to be German. Similarly as regards the Communistic governments of Russia, Jugoslavia, and China. If those peoples should want that type of government it is none of our business. But if these governments force that ideology on other peoples then it is our business. And not only if it is a threat to us. If it was our lend-lease and betrayals at Yalta and elsewhere that enabled the Communists to enslave peoples, such as half of Germany, Poland, Hungary, etc.,

— 46 —

(42)
"The Future Strength of Germany"

146 Davis Court, San Antonio, Texas
January, 1945

TO WHOM IT MAY CONCERN:

At last an article has appeared in an American magazine which correctly analyzes the source of the so-called German "problem" and disposes of most of the prescriptions for solving it. Everyone ought to read "The Future Strength of Germany," by Cary Byers, pen name of a Washington official, in *Harper's Magazine*, December, 1944, pp. 48-57.

The writer shows that the German problem consists of the fact that the Germans, owing to their science, efficiency, unity, and size, are intrinsically the greatest power in Europe but that Britain and now America and Russia refuse to allow her the influence commensurate with her real power. Here are some significant quotations:

"German aggression in international relations is not a creature of the Nazi party. The party rather is an expression of a deep-seated, though not necessarily ineradicable, national will toward dominance of Europe" (p.56). [One notes here that the writer does not say dominance of, or conquest of the WORLD, as the destroyer-dealers and the lendleasers used to scream.]

"A peaceful, democratic Germany is not an unattainable objective. Some of today's most conspicuously law-abiding nations are former aggressors. None of them, however, was cured by the application of psychiatric methods to international politics. Some were tamed by attaining positions in the world commensurate with their underlying strength. Others lost their underlying strength. There is no firmer law of national behavior than the one which induces a nation to seek to make its position in the world equal its real power. When the power basis for conquest goes, the psychological drive for conquest goes with it" (p.56).

"Few Swedes today would take seriously any suggestion that Sweden's former position be restored. That millions of Germans are receptive to comparable appeals does not mean that Germans are inherently more bloodthirsty or more gullible. It means that they have a better basis for hope of conquest than Swedes have" (p.57).

"Germany's real power, resting upon pre-eminence over its neighbors in heavy industry, population, geographical position, military skill and administrative ability, seems to a German to entitle his country to exercise a commensurate political dominance" (p.57). [One notes here that we Americans, owing to our similar real power, have in the Monroe Doctrine insisted and obtained such dominance in the whole Western Hemisphere—which explains our present bullying of Argentina.]

"The Americans, the Russians, and the British, for perfectly valid reasons of their own security, do not intend to permit Germany to register its real power by occupying a dominant political position in Europe. Germany will keep trying, however, just as long as the gap remains between her underlying power and her political position."

The writer advises that if Russia, for example, were helped to become really the most powerful nation in Europe, the German problem would be ended. One notes here that it would indeed. Then the Russians would dominate Europe. Can't we be realistic and just enough to let each people have as much to say as its intrinsic power entitles it to? Have we in this hemisphere the right to say with bombs who in Europe shall have the most to say?

Austin J. App, Ph.D.

---

then it becomes our moral duty to use all our moral, diplomatic, and economic powers to liberate them, even at the risk of war. In a war we would have the right to kill Russians or Chinese Communists only as long as they hold territories not their own and subjugate peoples against their will. Unconditional Surrender, killing on account of ideology, killing to force our type of government on them would be as immoral as these policies were against Germany, where they lost the peace, as every honorable person could have foreseen!

— 47 —

Just What are we Fighting for?

146 Davis Court, San Antonio 2, Texas
January 24, 1945

Time Magazine
330 East 22nd Street
Chicago 16, Ill.

To the Editor:

In your January 15 issue you rightly ask "what for?" What are we fighting for?

If for three years the senators, the generals, the columnists, and the cabinet officers of a large country cannot come to agree on the reason for a thing, wouldn't one then sensibly conclude that there simply is no good reason?

In Laurence Housman's *Victoria Regina,* Lord Beaconsfield says, "When the British nation goes to war, Madam, it ceases to listen to reason."

If after three years of killing and being killed in Europe, we still do not know what we are fighting for, isn't it about time to come to the only reasonable conclusion, namely,

Our boys do not know what they are fighting for,
because there is no reason for their fighting!

Sincerely,

Austin J. App, Ph.D.

Forbidding German POW's Native Salute

316 San Pedro Ave., San Antonio, Texas
May 5, 1945

Major Claude C. Wilde,
Commander, Prisoner of War Camp
Fort Sam Houston,
San Antonio, Texas

My dear Major Wilde:

A newspaper report of May 2 stated that you ordered German prisoners of war to renounce their native German military salute under penalty of death by starvation.

While I realize that you yourself gave the order under orders, I wonder whether you could give me information on the following three points or refer me to the department which can. The questions are:

1) Is forbidding prisoners of war the use of their native and customary military salute in accordance with the Geneva Conventions on handling prisoners?

2) Is starving prisoners of war for refusing to drop their country's salute in accordance with the Geneva Regulations or other international code?

3) Have the military or governmental authorities in Germany forbidden our soldiers our American salute?

As a college teacher and frequent writer and lecturer I ought to have the answers to these points, and I would greatly appreciate it if you could help me in this matter.

Very sincerely yours,

Austin J. App, Ph.D.

* Identical letter was sent to
   Col. Robert J. Saxon,
   Commander, Camp Brady
   San Angelo, Texas

●•■

(45)

Admiral Halsey on Murdering "Japs"

316 San Pedro, San Antonio 1, Texas
May 15, 1945

Time
330 East 22nd Street,
Chicago, Ill.

To the Editor:

In your April 30 issue you printed several pages of so-called German atrocities. And you also printed one item to show that We Americans, given the chance and excuse, are capable of the worst atrocities we allege against others.

Since you print the atrocity stories, I do hope you will also print this. In war both sides commit atrocities. In World War I both sides were finally proven to have shared shame about equally. It was also proven that the atrocities did not do the great harm. The harm was done by the atrocity stories. It was atrocity stories that made the British burn Joan of Arc at the stake as a war criminal. It was the atrocity stories that made Americans tolerate the scrapping of the just Fourteen Points for the greatest of all atrocities—the Versailles Treaty, which violated virtually every canon of justice.

Now you quote one of our great admirals, William F. Halsey. He wants to kill two Japanese officers, without trial or charge, for every American prisoner who died after Bataan. The Germans, in accordance with our own laws, executed everybody at Lidice who gave aid to political murderers. And we pretended horror—and cried atrocity. Now Admiral Halsey wants to murder two Japanese officers for every American prisoner lost, two Japanese officers who had absolutely nothing to do with the case! I beg you to tell us if any equally responsible German has ever expressed an atrocity principle as great as our own Admiral Halsey's. Give our Morgenthaus and Halseys just a little more time and they will get around to insisting that for every American killed or wounded in the war our boys must rape every German and Japanese girl!

Sincerely,

Austin J. App, Ph.D.

* Copies to Admiral Halsey and President Truman

(46)

A Phony "Catholic" Committee of Vengeance Seekers

316 San Pedro, San Antonio 1, Texas
May 16, 1945

Tablet
1 Hanson Place
Brooklyn 17, N.Y.

To the Editor:

Every Christian-minded reader will approve of Arthur J. Knowles' column, "Our Lay Theologians," and A. Cowan's letter, condemning the Committee of Catholic Laymen, headed by Emmanuel Chapman, convert from Judaism, for advocating German slave labor.

When a group of alleged Catholics, calling themselves a "Committee of Catholics for Human Rights," advocates slave labor for members of a defeated nation and further states that all members of a nation, whose government is declared guilty of starting a war, "should be liable to prosecution and punishment," then one has to vomit at the depths to which the Old Testament revenge spirit, the eye-for-an-eye dispensation can sink. Whatever the members of that Committee voting in favor of these barbarisms call themselves nominally, they are not Catholics and not Christians. They may think they are. Judas thought he was, too. But they aren't.

A Christian is one who knows that putting Americans of Japanese descent into concentration (relocation) camps is as bad in principle as putting Germans of Jewish descent into concentration camps. He realizes that if one constitutes a punishable war crime then the other does too, and only then.

It's about time everybody started being a little fair and just. Especially should people who presume to talk about "human rights" begin to realize that "human rights" include, not only one sect or nationality, but all sects, nationalities and races.

As for war criminals, some Christian rules must apply:

1) There must be no question of merely German or Japanese war criminals. It must be a question of WAR CRIMINALS—and war criminals of all nations must be treated by the same rules. A German, an American, a French, a Russian, a Japanese soldier who commits rape, robbery, murder must be treated the same way. And politically, the attack on Finland must be treated exactly as the attack on Poland. One nation's treatment of its nationals must be treated exactly like another's: the Russian murder of three million kulaks (*Time,* Feb. 5, 1945), the German incarceration of Jews, the American "relocation" of Japanese-Americans.

2) Only the person found guilty of a crime may be punished, not his sister, or mother, or brother, or anybody else at all. (Admiral Halsey's proposition to kill any two Japanese officers for every American prisoner maltreated staggers the mind in its atrociousness.)

3) If according to Msgr. John A. Ryan war crime trials may not be vindictive or vengeful but must serve the purpose of preventing a repetition of the crimes, then sound sociology and history, and obviously sound Christianity will warn us that executing so-called war criminals is not an act of wisdom but rather the last gasp of the lust for blood produced by a war.

The savages used to eat their war criminals—and, in agreement with

— 50 —

Emmanuel Chapman's Committee they ate the whole defeated people—
men, women, and children. Later, the chief war criminals were merely
burned at the stake—Joan of Arc is the great example. In between those
periods they used to crucify them!

Austin J. App, Ph.D.
Incarnate Word College

---

(47)

The Honorable Policy for German Emigres

316 San Pedro Ave., San Antonio 1, Texas
June 1, 1945

Mr. Heinrich Bruening
Harvard University
Cambridge, Mass.

Dear Mr. Bruening:

For the last few days International News Service has been publishing
interviews with German or so-called German emigres as to "Can Germany
Be Cured?"

Since all the interviewees seemed to be actuated by a blind Old-Testa-
ment eye-for-an-eye revenge sadism, I looked forward with apprehension
to the announced interview with you—for I have always respected you
as a real Christian.

It was with relief that I read this morning that you refused to comment as to what is to be done with Germany. At least you did not stoop
to the sadism or stupidity of the average emigre.

Naturally I wish you would have gone a little farther and said with
Bernard Shaw, "Treat the Germans decently and they'll be all right."

Germany committed crimes and mistakes—but I simply cannot see
where she committed any that other nations did not commit or under similar circumstances would have committed. Every person with sense and
influence ought to keep insisting on that. E.g. Germans imprisoned Jews
without trial: we, when we believed ourselves in a crisis, did so to Americans of Japanese descent—had these been as obstinate as the Jews in
Germany we conceivably would have killed them the same way.

Secondly, every American with sense and certainly every German
ought to insist that whatever crimes Germany committed, she did no
harm whatever to America—and to say she would have had she had the
chance is an unarguable assumption. We lendleased and destroyer dealt
ourselves against her—she did nothing to us.

Thirdly, every German when asked ought to say that whatever mistakes and crimes Germany committed the Allied side committed at least
as many. E.g. Russia attacks Poland; purges kulaks; we imprison
Nisei, etc.

Fourthly, however stupid it was, to use force at Danzig and in a deep
Christian sense wrong, the fact remains Danzig by every law of justice
and self-determination ought to have been incorporated into Germany.
If it was wrong to get Danzig its self-determined wish by force, it was
still more wrong on the part of France and England to prevent it by force.

These are things I believe men like you should suggest and convey.
Otherwise there will never be a just peace. A little boldness on the part

— 51 —

of men like you can sometimes check the sadistic tide of injustice and stupidity.

I take the liberty of including a few of my articles. I hope you will have time to read them. Thank you.

Austin J. App, Ph.D.

————————

(48)

Austrian Right to Union with Germany

114 Calle de Alfonso Herrera
Mexico, D.F., July 21, 1945

The Commonweal
386 Fourth Avenue
New York City

To the Editors:

After reading Ernst Karl Winter's valuable article on "Austrian Reconstruction," I beg you to print the following principles by which, I deeply feel, the Austrian problem must finally be settled: It will be recalled that Austria twice, before Hitler came to power in Germany, attempted union or Anschluss with Germany.

In all territorial problems three principles ought to be obeyed as axioms. First, the policy of power politics must not be invoked. Power politics, the vice and the curse that has made history a roll call of bloody wars, is the policy whereby nations oppose or enforce a move by another nation, not because that move is wrong or right, but because it will make a rival stronger or weaker. If Germany had opposed the voluntary union of Texas and the United States because such a union increased America's relative power potential over Germany, she would have been guilty of a piece of intolerable power politics which Americans and Texans would sooner or later have died for as at Bataan to circumvent.

Second, Wilson's obviously Christian principle of self-determination, pledged virtually by all the United Nations in the Atlantic Charter's "desire to see no territorial changes that do not accord with the expressed wishes of the people concerned," must be applied honestly and decisively.

Thirdly, separatism among peoples culturally and economically related is reactionary and un-christian; federalization or unionism among peoples culturally and economically related is progressive, is the motion of Christian brotherhood, and is, however impeded, ultimately unpreventable. However long it took, New Yorker and Virginian, Bavarian and Prussian, finally federated; and by however many stupidities and injustices prevented, at long last someday North Irishman and South Irishman will federate, and North German and South German.

Specifically the only just principles for handling Austria are:

1. If the majority of the people of Austria, determined as honestly as possible, want to be independent, they must be allowed and helped to be so. (Nations should federate when they are ready: they must never be clubbed into federating.)

2. If the majority of the people of Austria, determined as honestly as possible, want to be federated with Germany they must be allowed and helped to do so.

3. If the proponents of German dismemberment in order to reconstitute an independent Austria are as certain as they claim of the Austrian will to independence they have nothing to lose by a fair plebiscite or similar device.

4. If proponents of Austrian independence fear that an honest plebiscite might endanger the Reformation-born 400-year-old fratricidal split in the German peoples of Central Europe, then they are simply the same old ugly power politicians whose activities Wilson condemned (Feb. 11, 1918) when he declared "that peoples and provinces are not to be bartered about from sovereignty to sovereignty as if they were chattels or powers in a game, even the great game, now forever discredited, of the balance of power."

Sincerely,

Austin J. App, Ph.D.

————•——

(49)

Vansittart Calls Germans "Savages"

114 Calle de Alfonso Herrera
Mexico, D.F., July 25, 1945

Time
330 East 22nd St.,
Chicago, Illinois
Sirs:

In your account of Lord Vansittart you rightly report how he wants the Germans called savages since the time of the Frederick the Great but not since the time when the Romans first called them savages. That is a laugh! Of course Vansittart does not want the Germans called savages that early. Because that early the Anglo-Saxons, the future Englishmen, were still in the middle of Europe, the fiercest of the German tribes. Later these set up shop in England, enslaved the Irish and the Hindus and conquered one-fifth of the world, while their comparatively peaceful brothers behind in central Europe conquered nothing, though it is true that Prussians, Rhinelanders, Danzigers, Bavarians, and Austrians have for a hundred years now vainly argued and sometimes fought for the privilege of uniting as one nation. Eventually they will be so united—but unfortunately too late for all the brother-splitting Vansittarts to recognize their crime and their ultimate futility.

Ausin J. App, Ph.D.

————•——

(50)

Allies of Stalin — and Franco

114 Calle de Alfonso Herrera
Mexico, D.F., July 30, 1945

The New Republic
40 Eas 49th Street,
New York 17, N.Y.
To the Editors:

In your July 2 issue you recommend treating Franco as a war criminal because "he gave all possible aid to Hitler and Mussolini, and only failed to enter the war on the Axis side because he didn't dare to." For one thing, if Franco had given "all possible aid to Hitler" he would have marched into France in 1940 as Stalin marched into Poland in 1939.

Your attitude towards the Negro, the Nisei, towards the Morgenthau de-industrialization plan, all these make me want to think of you as honest and honorable men. I have read some of your books (George Soule, Stark Young, Alfred Kazin).

— 53 —

I ask you, therefore, as one who hates to think all men the "odious vermin" Swift speaks of, how you as allies of Stalin, who as an ally of Hitler attacked and took a slice of Poland, who twice ruthlessly attacked and quartered Finland, who absorbed three republics, who slaughtered virtually all clerics in Russia, who starved four million Ukrainians to death (according to *Time* Magazine statistics), who daily deports thousands of helpless non-Communists to Siberia, I ask how you, as allies of Stalin, can in conscience talk of Franco as a war criminal. Gentlemen, how can you? Is Robert M. Hutchins the only American in whom the beastliness of war has not destroyed all honor and honesty? I ask you honestly how an ally of Stalin can throw stones at Franco.

Sincerely,

Austin J. App, Ph.D.

---

(51)

Atrocities in Central Europe
Consequence of Unconditional Surrender

316 San Pedro Ave., San Antonio 1, Texas
September 5, 1945

Mr. F. P. Kenkel
Social Justice Review
3835 Westminster Place
St. Louis 8, Mo.

Dear Mr. Kenkel:

I have just finished reading your "A Ferocious Aspect," in September's Social Justice Review, a title with which you happily designate the mass expropriation and expulsion of twelve million people of Eastern Europe from their homelands.

Last week I returned from three months in Mexico and have spent this time reading back numbers of papers. When I noticed all the bestial and atrocious peace proposals and occupation rules and the apparent approval if not glee with which the American press reported all of them, even to the reports of the looting and raping which Russians practiced against Germans and Hungarians and even to their rules of shooting fifty hostages for every incident no matter how caused by these people, I was so sickened that I could practically not eat or sleep. It seemed too much even for me to believe.

I say even for me. Because I maintained all along that American intervention had nothing whatever to do with idealism or Nazism but simply with what the Morgenthau-Baruch plan now proves—a bloody lust to eliminate the only people which is NOT BAD ENOUGH but civilized enough to be a competent competitor industrially and commercially of Britain and America. I have all along maintained that if Christ had been president of Germany, Christ would have had to ask that the Danzigers be given their self-determination and Roosevelt and all the interventionists would just as surely have opposed Christ's rectification of the Versailles crimes as they opposed them in the case of Hitler. The many faults of the Nazi regime were no greater than those of dozens of other countries and much less than those of Russia. These faults were merely played up in order to have a satanically clever excuse to make the injustices of Versailles stick in a still dirtier form for another thirty years.

I maintained all along that Unconditional Surrender was simply and only an atrociously unjust device in order to destroy Germany industrially

— 54 —

and commercially. Allies of Stalin had no honest excuse for not negotiating with Hitler. And the Atlantic Charter with its "After the destruction of Nazi aggression" was from the beginning only a hypocritical swindle to make professors, grandmothers and clergymen swallow the war as a crusade.

The proposed territorial robberies, the deindustrialization of Germany ——all in violent and' obvious destruction of the Atlantic Charter—simply prove what a swindle our intervention was. We fought Germany not because she was bad but because she was so highly civilized as to be our only efficient industrial and commercial competitor.

As I said, I was therefore prepared for nearly every kind of injustice and atrocity following Unconditional Surrender, a policy which itself was a greater atrocity than any attributed to Hitler.

But believe me even all my cynicism and expectancy of the worst was not prepared for the master crimes of history embodied in Yalta and Potsdam—tearing obvious provinces from their motherland, and then throwing its people out of their homes and possessions and driving them like cattle to foreign lands, lands where all the houses have been bombed to pieces by the idealistic Atlantic Charterites and where starvation not only exists but is something almost gloated over by even such people as Mrs. Roosevelt (for whom I always had a lingering respect.)

I have been therefore completely dejected. I had not believed that mankind, Atlantic Charterized mankind at that, could be so bestial and barbarous.

Consequently when I read your article calling the expulsion of these people from their homes a ferocious act, I breathed up just a little—at least a few people are not savages and bloodthirsty Morganthauistic beasts.

Congratulations on that article. It is learned, it is sound, it is strong, it is dignified.

But it needs to be hammered at the world.

I hereby formally ask you to send a reprint of it to all cabinet members and all senators and if possible to as many congressmen as you can —for a check of five dollars I inclose for the purpose. The check is sent for that purpose—reprints not copies, reprints go farther and are read more carefully—for your sending reprints of your article to as many from the top down as the five dollars will pay for.

Let me know if you are doing it. This shameful atrocity, this enormous torture and hardship inflicted on the world, on millions of people, must be stopped. We must all work at it. Keep at it in the magazine. Quote the Pope or rather article "International Orientation" in *Osser Romano,* about Aug. 30, as follows: "It is contrary to the law of nature to remove million and millions of persons from their homes" etc. Perfect for quote—2 paragraphs.

Compliments also on the excerpts from Hutchins' speech—that was the best excerpt. One must prove to our beast-minded people that all human beings are sinners and that atrocities must have absolutely nothing to do with peace proposals—must not be made a filthy excuse for violating the Atlantic Charter. In any case, reading carefully everything possible and between the lines I am sadly convinced that Allied occupation troops have in four months committed more rape than the Germans in four years.

Well, let me know if you got reprints of your article to the President, cabinet, and senators.

Sincerely,

Austin J. App, PhD.

Bishops should Protest the Crimes of Potsdam

316 San Pedro Avenue
San Antonio 1, Texas
October 13, 1945

Most Rev. Aloysius J. Muench
608 Broadway
Fargo, North Dakota

Your Excellency:

I was inexpressibly happy that you approved of my summary of your noble Lenten Pastoral.

Since your kind letter of March 15 I have spent three months in Mexico. Surely in the last four months the concept and purpose of a just peace have deteriorated to a level of barbarism not even the most pessimistic of us imagined possible. History had of course convinced me that refusal to negotiate a peace and, horrors of horrors, insistence on unconditional surrender were the certain road to an unjust peace, to another Versailles betrayal of war intervention idealism. But I did not believe it possible for our statesmen to be so morally depraved as to sanction (1) the transfer from Germany to Russia and Poland of such obviously and ancient German territories as East Prussia, Pomerania, Silesia, (2) the forcible expulsion from their homelands of some ten million peoples having lived in these territories for centuries, and (3) the unashamed and brutal confiscation of all the real possessions (homes, cattle, furniture) of the families living in the territories being torn from Germany in flagrant and obvious violation of the Atlantic Charter and Wilson's Fourteen Points. Point Three I had not even envisaged; I had not even adverted to it; it is a new atrocity in history—even the evicted Acadians were somewhat compensated by the British. All this, I insist, represents a perversion of justice beyond what any Christian would have believed possible even a few years ago.

For this horrible peace debacle I do not only blame the politicians but also those often well-meaning men who insisted that one could not negotiate a peace with the enemy and had to insist on dictating a peace or even unconditional surrender. That means many of our fellow Catholics and even of your fellow members of the hierarchy heavily share the responsibility for the peace atrocities which many of us explained would follow a policy of unconditional surrender.

The fearful suspicion is developing in me that this whole war was more an attack upon Catholic Europe than upon Nazi or fascistic Europe. Otherwise how could Allies of Stalin try to foment war against Spain or speak of Franco as a war criminal. Under the smokescreen of rooting out Naziism, Germany is looted and robbed and private property is destroyed. When will the NCWC recognize this and speak out against it as loud as it formerly spoke out for bombing and slaughtering eighty million Germans, including thirty million Catholics, into Unconditional Surrender?

There are several honestly peaceloving and impartially just members of the hierarchy in the country. Among these you are the leader by virtue of knowledge, ability, and true love of justice. And if you don't take a strong lead, there will not be any action that is thoroughgoingly just.

Might it not be possible for you to organize at least some of the members of the hierarchy to issue a strong, unequivocal statement against the three injustices I cited above? You remember when the Bishops spoke last, demanding adherence to the Atlantic Charter, while such adherence was not achieved in fact, yet immediately the government here and at Yalta felt it necessary at least to give lip service to it. I am convinced that the world, while it will never listen fully to anybody who speaks for justice, will yet not sink quite so low and barbarously against justice when the Pope and when bishops speak out CLEARLY for a point or points than it would sink otherwise. I consider it the duty of the hierarchy so to speak out whenever governments are about to violate against obvious justice or have done so. The business of Christians, I take it, is not to get along in this world but to use all their moral force (as distinct from physical —war and bloodshed advocating force) to try to make men and their governments conform to reason and the will of God. You have done so. I just wonder whether you could not perhaps make another attempt to have the Catholic hierarchy speak out so strongly and so SPECIFICALLY for a just, Atlantic Charter peace that at least some of the contemplated injustices will be moderated.

Under separate cover I send you two Sunday Visitor articles, one on territorial injustices, the other on the mass expulsion of East European Germans. Obviously what holds for Germany holds for Hungary and Austria and Finland. Also for Japan, though, because Japan is pagan, she is, thank heavens, not treated quite so shamefully and brutally as Catholic and Protestant Germany and Catholic Hungary and Catholic Austria. As I said before, I am becoming convinced that all this brutality and injustice is more an assault upon Christianity, especially Catholicism, than it is on Naziism. Nazism is defeated and destroyed, why then continue de-industrialization, expulsions, lootings, and starvations? Why not return German prisoners, etc.?

I am also sending you a Christian Pacifist article. I realize you do not take such a view. Nevertheless, I am so convinced that that way lies true Christianity that I hope you will not be too unsympathetic towards my position. It will need, of course, many more thousand words to present Christian pacifism adequately.

A Sister, who is an admirer of you, recently gave me a fine mounted picture of you which she found in a magazine. I can see it from my desk.

May I say again, I know you are an extraordinarily busy man and I realize fully my presumption in writing and sending you article copies. I beg you again, therefore, not to feel any need of acknowledging any copies I send you. I hope you are well.

Yours very sincerely,

Austin J. App

(53)

Winchell Keeps Speaking of "Verminy"

316 San Pedro, San Antonio 1, Texas
October 17, 1945

The Tablet
1 Hanson Pl.
Brooklyn, N.Y.
To the Editor:

According to *Time,* October 8, 1945, General Eisenhower reports to Congress that in Germany "Less than 10% of the industry in the U.S. sector is working," and that "The average German diet was one-third below subsistence level." That means that Germans are getting one-third less than is necessary for them not slowly to starve to death. The destruction of German industry is a result of the Morgenthau plan, strongly endorsed and probably inspired by Bernard Baruch who, as reported June 22, 1945, admitted before a Senate investigation committee that his 14-point plan to strangle Germany means "that the Reich citizens will suffer hunger and want."

In spite of this seeming calculated extermination-starving of the German people, Walter Winchell complains that "Our namby-pambying in Verminy has sickened American reporters there" (*San Antonio Light,* Oct. 17, 1945), and continues speaking of Germany, the land of Faulhaber, Niemöller, and Preysing, as *Verminy.*

I considered it an act of charity, therefore, today to send him the following little note of advice:

> My dear Mr. Winchell:
>
> *If you don't stop calling Germany "Verminy," which is a land in which live twenty-five million Catholics and many fine Lutherans, you will find that many good people who have always protected Jews will begin calling the land of your ancestors "Kikestine." I think it would be better if you treated all Germans the way you want all Germans to treat you and your race. Blood-thirsty revenge nastiness like yours sooner or later boomerangs*

Since men like Mr. Morgenthau and Mr. Baruch might like this advice too, perhaps you could publish this letter.

Sincerely yours,

Austin J. App, Ph.D.

————————<•>————————

(54)

Just War Crimes Trials Must Try Crimes of Both Sides

316 San Pedro Ave., San Antonio 1, Texas
October 20, 1945

Dr. William Draper Lewis
American Law Institute
Philadelphia, Pa.

Mr dear Dr. Lewis:

Your article on Justice in the current *American-German Review* is most interesting and stimulating. You are making, it seems to me a tremendous step forward when you recognize that what the people mean by justice is really revenge—". . . it was natural to adopt a religious or moral reason for the punishment, even though the punishment was primarily due to anger at harm done."

The desire so to punish the loser in any war is therefore simply the old savage instinct which formerly always ended in the literal eating of the conquered and the rape and enslavement of their women. Since Christianity opposes this, the old beast in men, in the winners of a war, has to prostitute religion into a justification of the same revenge instincts—by playing up the various and invariable crimes committed by the losers in a war and hushing up the same crimes committed by the winners.

The present allied trials of so-called war criminals on the losing side is a civilizing step and is a step made along the usual hypocritical road to progress. Obviously, when the accusers both try and also condemn, it is not justice and it is not really a trial. Only if neutrals were doing the trying and the condemning and each side could name the war criminals of the other could one speak of justice. Bernard Shaw sees this clearly and said so. Other Christians too will eventually see it.

In the meanwhile it is good to see you say that the standard of right and wrong must be the Golden rule—Do unto others as you would have done to yourself. You also happily stress the need for impartiality . . . "that they may truly and impartially administer . . ."

In this spirit you ask the German so-called offenders, those who put Germans of Jewish descent into concentration camps because of their race, etc., be quickly tried. All that is needed, in the interest of impartiality and justice, is that all war criminals of both sides be so tried, e.g. just as the Germans who put Germans of Jewish descent into concentration camps because of their race should be tried so Americans who put Americans of Japanese descent into concentration (relocation) camps because of their race must be tried; just as Hitler was to have been tried for attacking Poland (to rectify the self-determination principle violated at Versailles regarding Danzig) so Stalin must be tried for invading Finland (without any justification at all); just as Germans who raped and looted must be tried so the troops under General Eisenhower who raped 2000 Stuttgart girls in one weekend and hundreds of others since and the Russians, who according to British Archbishop Griffin raped 100,000 girls in Vienna alone and who by universally admitted reports looted and pillaged everything from machines to furniture in Germany must be tried and if found guilty treated just as you say, according to the Golden Rule and impartial justice, Germans must be treated.

And all this as you say should be done directly and immediately—impartiality requires this uniform application of justice to all sides. Otherwise the impression might be created that the losers are the only ones who committed atrocities and so seem to give justification to the greatest of atrocities the Big Three are committing namely:

1) Partitioning three or four provinces away from Germany against the clear demand of the Atlantic Charter that no provinces are to be bartered about unless the people living there want it and it is for their benefit.

2) Expelling forcibly some ten million people whose provinces have been so atrociously robbed against the principles of common sense, universal justice and the specific Fourteen Points and Atlantic Charter.

3) Not only expelling ten millions of people from their ancient homelands but, in what is, according to Churchill "a tragedy on a prodigious scale" robbing them literally of house and home, of their farms, houses, furniture, cattle, and even most of their clothes.

These latter three crimes are greater than any so far committed in history—at least they are on a vaster scale. To prevent their being completely carried out trials of the criminals responsible for these three mass atrocities ought to begin immediately, simultaneously with those of Tojo, Goering and Ribbentrop.

I hope you will, embued as you are with the spirit of the Golden Rule and the sense of impartiality, try hard to lift us above the savage and brute stage in this matter which in all ages has punished only the losers and will insist that the war criminals of both sides will be tried and punished in exactly the same manner and by the same rules.

Thank you again for an article which gave me a lot to think about.

Sincerely yours,

Austin J. App, Ph.D.
Incarnate Word College
San Antonio 1, Texas

Copy to Editor of American-German Review.

(55)

Bertrand Russell Moralizes About Franco

316 San Pedro, San Antonio 1, Texas
November 2, 1945

Brooklyn *Tablet*
1 Hanson Place
Brooklyn, New York
To the Editor:

In the "Good Old Days" I used to think the power of old Satan was grossly exaggerated. But the way in this war seemingly good people called things an atrocity when the Axis did it and a stroke of glorious justice when the Allies do it greatly shook my former convictions, e.g. when the German made off with French museum pieces it was looting, but when the Allies cart off whole factories it is reparations!

But what drives Father Furfey's book, *The Mystery of Iniquity* most sharply home to me, and makes me feel bitterly that there must be such a thing as a satanic influence in the world is the way many so-called thinkers and self-confessed honest men weigh Stalin's Russia and Franco's Spain in the balance and find Stalin a lamb and Franco a wolf.

So advises Bertrand Russell as to what America and England should do:

> The first thing is a vigorous and militant championship of democracy in all regions outside the Russian sphere of influence. This should apply, in the first instance, to Western Europe, including Spain, where Franco should no longer be tolerated.

Then after declaring that Franco, because he is allegedly undemocratic must therefore be agitated or bombed out, Mr. Russell (in his article very fine in many other respects) says:

> The Russian government is opposed to capitalism and democracy; it follows that, if there is to be genuine co-operation between Russia and America, each must acknowledge the right of the other to its own system in its own sphere of influence. (See *Common Sense,* October, 1945, p. 5).

Can anyone consider such reasoning as *not satanic* but *merely human?*

Austin J. App, Ph.D.

—◆◆—

(56)

The Vengefulness of Non-Christian Emigres

November 18, 1945

Dear Father Hans A. Reinhold:

Thanks for your November 8th letter.

The figures of the rape of Viennese women are those of British Archbishop Griffin as he gave them on his return from Germany and Austria—100,000 Viennese girls raped not once but many times, he says.

I have read all reports available carefully and I say sadly but firmly that Allied occupation troops have committed more rape and loot in four months than German occupation troops committed in four years—in fact German troops except in the inevitable isolated cases did not commit rape, nor loot in the military sense of the word.

My alluding to a similarity of name to Morganthau was just a bit playful. What I meant to suggest was that fellows like Emil Ludwig when they want to damn all Germans call themselves and have themselves announced as Germans and say in effect: See, I am a German myself and if

— 60 —

I say all Germans are bad it must be so—if I say Germany must be crushed forever who could know better than a fellow, if escaped, German. Then when one says to them that they themselves ought to be punished with the rest of the Germans they suddenly change their tune and say, "Oh, but I was not a German; I was not responsible for Germany's crimes; I am a Jew."

I want them to stop having it both ways. Also I want them to remember that starving a German is as bad as starving a Jew. And if all Germans are to be looted, starved and raped for having put Jews into concentration camps then all Americans deserve the same fate for having put Americans of Japanese descent into concentration camps.

In my letter to you I meant to imply that apparently you considered yourself a German of German descent or an American of German descent when there is blame as well as when there is praise. I meant to compliment you. If the Americans of Japanese descent whom we put in concentration camps acted the way the refugee Ludwigs and the Americans of Jewish descent like Winchell and Morganthau act, we would call them bestial. I say the Ludwigs and the Morgenthaus are acting like beasts towards Germany and Germans. I was glad from your letter to see that you, though apparently a German refugee, have remained Christian and have not become bestial.

As for supporting my stand, if you have the Christian spirit you will, along with the Atlantic Charter, damn the bartering of territories against the will of the people, including East Prussia; you will also damn the expulsion of the people there; you will shudder in horror at looting them of all their property. If you have this Christian spirit you are on my side. You can't be otherwise. I want justice—do to others as you want done by for everybody—all nationalities, all nations, all races, and all religions. I believe you are such a Christian or close to it. There are few left. They must stick together. The gulf between decent-minded people and the beast-minded ones making this peace does not permit the decent-minded ones to quarrel over details. Thanks again for your letter. My letter was meant as a compliment—so is this. By and by I'll send you other articles.

Sincerely

Austin J. App, Ph.D.

(57)

The Robbing, Looting, and Expelling by the Victors

November 20, 1945

Rev. Harold C. Gardiner, S.J.
America

Dear Father Gardiner:

Your recent article in *America,* "Germany Must Be Fed" was excellent; so was the unsigned, "Death March from Silesia."

It is good to see *America* step forth to indicate the brutal tragedy in Christian Europe the Yalta and Potsdam peacemakers have perpetrated.

Yes, our holy interventionistic crusaders have ended by robbing and looting twelve million people out of house and home and even some of the clothes off their backs, have driven them like unwanted beasts out of their ancient territories and homeland, have made good progress in starving them to death, have exposed a large number of them to rape, and have furthermore handed large sections of Christian Europe over to the Red Terror to loot and rape at their wish—100,000 in Vienna alone.

— 61 —

These are the accomplishments of the Big Three who are trying the Germans as war criminals.

It is high time that that portion of the press which still pretends to justice and Christianity start trying to check the bestial terrors our policies of unconditional surrender and Morganthauism unloosed. Thank you for making such a start.

Sincerely,

Austin J. App, Ph.D.

⚫

(58)

The Crime Against the Sudeten Germans

316 San Pedro, San Antonio 1, Texas
February 24, 1946

Our Sunday Visitor
Huntingdon, Indiana

To the Editor:

I am profoundly grateful to Father Placid Sasek, of St. Procopius Abbey, for explaining in your February 24 issue that the Czech Benedictines who took over the Brunau Abbey, from which the Czech government had expelled the Sudeten monks, did not do so to appropriate the monastery but to safekeep it for the expelled owners. This good intention on the part of the Czech Benedictines is a candle of Christianity in a whirlwind of barbarism.

From the news reports of the Czech expulsion of the Brunau monks and the taking over of the monastery by the Czech Benedictines, one could only conclude, as Father E. J. Reichenberger logically did, that these facts were identical with the government-published policy of robbing the three million-odd other Sudetens. Not the facts, but the intention, of which only Father Sasek and the newly installed monks could know, keep the Brunau case from being the robbery it looks. All honor to Father Sasek's Benedictines for being determined to prevent at least one robbery—and for trying to feed Czechs and Sudetens alike!

However, as to the treatment of the Sudetens by the Czech government, I beg to summarize the main points as reported first hand by Willy Brandt, well-known and reliable Norwegian reporter in the Norwegian press of December 1945 (reprinted in *Nord-Amerika,* Feb. 14, 1946):

1. The Sudetens (without distinction of politics) of any locality are given only several hours, sometimes only ten minutes, to get ready for deportation.
2. They may take along only 25 kilograms of belongings, including food for seven days, and 200 marks at the most. They are therefore completely robbed of house and home and furniture and cattle—and of their watches and jewels, save only their wedding ring.
3. At the border they are usually robbed of the small pack and the money still in their possession, even to the point of a second shirt and of their overcoats.
4. Usually they have to sleep face down in the open during their trek and are shot if they raise their head.
5. Those who protest the treatment or wander from an ordered spot are shot.
6. Willy Brandt adds, "Violation of women occurs constantly. In some cases the women were beaten senseless and then raped."

— 62 —

7. In one camp of which Brandt had personal knowledge "forty babies died in two days."

That is why the American bishops (Nov. 19, 1945) said, "The inhumanities which now mark the mass transference of populations . . . should have no place in our civilization."

But the root atrocity remains the very expulsion itself. The Sudetens were a third of Bohemia and a fifth of Czecho-Slovakia, when I traveled through there in 1931. There were, therefore, proportionately more Sudetens in Czecho-Slovakia than Catholics in America, and twice as many as there are Negroes in this country. If we permit the Sudetens, for purely racial reasons, to be expelled from their country and totally robbed, then Southerners can solve the "Negro" problem by deporting all Negroes to Africa, and Communists and KuKluxers can solve the "Catholic" problem by driving the twenty million Catholics into Mexico—and taking over their homes and farms. If we ever lose a war, the conqueror by the precedent we set at Potsdam, may do so!

I cannot beg every Catholic of whatever racial strain too urgently to condemn the expulsion of the twelve million Sudeten and Eastern Germans with all his vocal and financial energy as the most dangerous atrocity of modern times.

Sincerely,

Austin J. App, Ph.D.

Copies to E. J. Reichenberger and Rev. Placid Sasek.

(59)

Jews and Nisei Both Wronged for Same Reason

316 San Pedro, San Antonio 1, Texas
March 2, 1946

The American Mercury
570 Lexington Ave.
New York 22, N.Y.

Sir:

In your March issue Saul K. Padover asks the German Bishop of Aachen, "If the Bishop was so ardent a champion of the truth, why, then, did neither he nor his Church as a whole nor most decent Germans fight openly against the Nazi liars and murderers?"

Congresswoman Clare Booth Luce publicly declared that President Roosevelt lied us into the war. The German Bishop should have asked what Mr. Padover did about Roosevelt's lying us into the war!

He should also have asked what Mr. Padover and the rest of us did when the Rooseveltians put 110,000 Americans of Japanese descent for no crime except that they considered "the Japanese race an enemy race," as our General DeWitt said of them, as Hitler said of the Germans of Jewish descent?

The Bishop should also have asked what Mr. Padover did when troops under General Eisenhower's command raped 2000 Stuttgart girls and what he is doing about the Morgenthau Plan which has already killed more German babies than there ever were Jews in Germany?

It's easy to say what the German bishops should have done when

the Jews were persecuted. Emil Ludwig and Albert Einstein sneaked off
to safety and from behind American guns complain that the German
bishops did not get themselves martyred fighting for them where they
themselves fled from the fight.

Austin J. App, Ph.D.
Incarnate Word College
San Antonio 2, Texas

----

(60)

Plea to Protest Rape of East Prussia

Incarnate Word College
San Antonio 2, Texas
April 20, 1946

General Walter Krueger
509 Howard St.
San Antonio, Texas
My dear General Krueger:

The British magazine, the *Economist* (Dec. 15, 1945) calls the tearing
away of East Prussia and other eastern provinces from Germany "a
hideous injustice." It says, "In the East, the policy of truncation was
wrong—nothing can make it anything but a hideous injustice." (p. 852)

You are a great military hero of our country. You are feted everywhere and asked to make a few remarks.

You also spent your boyhood in East Prussia. Until the ruthless
robbery and expulsion of its people since you helped achieve an Allied Unconditional Surrender victory, you may have had some relatives there.

If even a British paper has the clearsightedness and the courage to
call the Allied treatment of East Prussia "a hideous injustice," don't you
think then that the great American General who knows East Prussia
better than any other American or Briton ought to speak out against the
"hideous injustice" that is wreaked against the province of his birth?

Justice is everybody's business. To do justice to East Prussia is as
important for us as it is for the Germans or the Russians. As a Christian
one must believe in the brotherhood of man. Injustice to the East Prussians is injustice to the human family, to you and to me.

And each of us must try to prevent or moderate such injustice. And
we must do it according to our abilities.

Your ability to become a champion for justice to the East Prussians,
and the defeated generally, is immense. You have won the highest laurels
on the battlefield, you can and should now win much nobler ones in the
field of humanity.

Surely you did not fight the war so your government could, after your
victory, inflict on the East Prussians the cruelest robbery and expulsion
in history? Well, if you say so, if you just say that whenever you are
asked to address a few words, it will ring around the world. All just-
minded people will immediately hail you gratefully and enthusiastically.
Some of the others will soon follow. And the rest should not matter to any
brave man.

In a few days I shall take the liberty of telephoning you. I herewith
inclose a reprint on "Territorial Injustices." I do hope you will consider
my addressing you as meant for the good of all of us—most of all, good
for the soldiers you commanded.

Sincerely yours,   *Austin J. App,* Ph.D.

According to General Krueger he was born in West Prussia, not East.—Editor.

— 64 —

Barbarous Indoctrination of German POW's

316 San Pedro, San Antonio 1, Texas

The Tablet
1 Hanson Place
Brooklyn, New York
To the Editor:

About the same time the German bishop's pastoral, asked to be withdrawn by our AMG, complained among other things that German prisoners of war had not been returned home, articles appeared in many of our magazines colorfully describing how our Army is indoctrinating German POW's in democracy behind barbed wires.

More than that, it seems the degree of indoctrination is made the yardstick of their eligibility for repatriation. We read, "some 300 of this particular class of 2,000 taking the course were not deserving of immediate return to Germany. They'd go back to their prison camps for further seasoning" (See *Colliers*, May 25, p. 42). "We send back to Germany only those who we believe are really democrats at heart," said Colonel Smith (*Ibid.*).

I wonder whether the Army and the people actually realize what this means. If we can keep Germans prisoners indefinitely unless they become so-called democrats, is not clear that Stalin is justified in holding his millions of Catholic and Lutheran Germans prisoners and slave-laborers until they become good communists? If he does so, will we then complain and point a holier-than-thou finger at the Bolsheviks?

Actually the policy of our authorities towards German prisoners of war is appallingly wrong and so weakens our moral position that it will eventually cause us great embarrassment.

In the first place, political indoctrination is a violation of the Geneva Convention. That is why the Army kept it secret until the Germans could not retaliate. Secondly, Article 75, of the Geneva Convention, declares, "When belligerents conclude a convention of armistice, they must, in principle, have appear therein stipulations regarding the repatriation of prisoners of war."

In the manner in which we imposed unconditional surrender we violated this principle. The Article goes on, "If it has not been possible to insert stipulations in this regard in such convention, belligerents shall nevertheless come to an agreement as soon as possible. In any case, repatriation of prisoners shall be effected with the least possible delay after the conclusion of peace."

The Germans surrendered a year ago. For us still to hold their prisoners is a crime—as the Pope in his Christmas allocution, the American bishops in their annual spring statement, and the German bishops in the "gagged" pastoral indicate. But when on top of that we stipulate for their return that they have become what we designate as good democrats we throw the world back to the time when princes thought they had a right to kill or enslave people for differing religions.

The Russians as unjustly as we hold, it is estimated, some 5,000,000 Germans as prisoners. By our example they have a right to hold them until they are good communists. That means about 2,000,000 Catholics have the choice of being damned and going home, or remaining faithful and rotting to death in Russian prisons. Do we want that? If not, then let's tell our government to send its German prisoners home now—and apologize to them for the past unjust imprisonment.

Austin J. App, Ph.D.

(62)

Jailing Germans for Telling the Truth

316 San Pedro, San Antonio 1, Texas
June 3, 1946

The Call
303 Fourth Avenue
New York 10, New York

Dear Sir:

Under "Burning Books Again," Norman Thomas in your May 20 issue describes how our AMG re-educators of Germany prosecute the Four Freedoms by burning books, destroying historical monuments, and forbidding rowing and skiing.

The day after, on May 21, an AP dispatch reported that the business manager of the Liberal Democratic party in Greater Hesse, American zone, was "sentenced to five years in prison today by an American military-government court." He "was accused of having said that Russian soldiers raped German women and having predicted 'a new war between America and Russia'" in which "Germany will fight on the western side."

Isn't there anybody in this country who can teach our interventionistic Four Freedom-ites what freedom of speech means? Shouldn't the AMG boys who put this German in jail be hurriedly put in jail themselves for applying methods worse than those we were lendleased into the war purportedly to fight against?

I use the word **worse** advisedly. I am convinced that if the Nazis during their French and other occupations had put everybody in jail who said, for example, that the Italians (German allies) raped Greek women (which would have been a lie, while the Russian raping is by now a world scandal) and that in the next war they (the French) would be on the German side, then the German concentration camps would have harbored ten times as many people as they did.

Respectfully yours,

Austin J. App, Ph.D.

———

(63)

Jews in Europe, How Many Slain?

Incarnate Word College
San Antonio 2, Texas
May 22, 1946

Time
Rockefeller Center
New York 20, New York

Gentlemen:

In your May issue you say that "Before Hitler, Europe's non-Russian Jewry numbered 6,500,000."

Since you have tremendous facilities for factfinding which an individual like me does not have, couldn't you be persuaded to make a thorough check of these figures.

They seem to be exaggerated. According to Almanacs there never were more than 15,000,000 Jews in the whole world—there appear to be as many now. Secondly, Wm. Shirer's *Berlin Diary* states somewhere that Germany never had more than about 700,000 Jews. And when Germany surrendered there still seemed to be about a half million there.

— 66 —

Time would do a useful service if once and for all it investigated all those figures thoroughly. Just how many Jews were executed and for what; how many died of abuse in concentration camps and for what; how many were said to have been killed when they simply died of old age.

And how many were in one way or another brought into the United States, Mexico, and Canada. An AP dispatch, Bremerhaven, May 11, states that the United states had rescued 3,000,000 refugees. Most of them appear to have been Jews, yet Judge Simon F. Rifkind recently stated that the Nazis slew 6,000,000 Jews. What are the facts?

A just peace depends to a large extent on facts and truth—about friend and enemy. I wish **Time** would really dig out and present the best available facts now. What we have heard regarding the Jewish population of Europe and its treatment is not substantiated fact.

Sincerely Yours,

Austin J. App, Ph.D.
Incarnate Word College
San Antonio, Texas

P.S.—If you want to print all or any part of this you may. But what I seriously want is a Time study of the facts.

(64)

Victors Blow Up More of Shelterless Germany

December 31, 1946

American Mercury
570 Lexington Ave
New York 22, N.Y.

To the Editor:

In the article, "Housing and Birth Control," (December, 1946), the University of Wisconsin is praised for providing housing for 4526 additional students by commandeering "an air-forces training field and a powder plant" and leasing trailers.

A powder plant could therefore be converted to needy housing.

At present the most freezingly shelterless people in the world are the Germans. Allied expulsions and Allied bombings have made tens of millions shelterless. Our authorities pretend to be interested in alleviating the sad condition and actually spend millions of taxpayer dollars in some sort of alleviating efforts.

In the meanwhile we read this item, headlined, "4 Powder Plants In Bavaria Go Up." AP reports, December 17, 1946, that "Four of the largest powder plants in Bavaria . . . were blown up Tuesday in the program to eliminate Germany's war potential."

What will future Germans whose parents froze to death and right-minded people everywhere think of the vandalism which, while converting powder plants at home to housing, blows up such plants in a country most of whose homes have been destroyed by Allied bombings and whose food supply has been destroyed by the Morgenthau Plan?

Sincerely,

Austin J. App, Ph.D.
Professor, Incarnate Word College
San Antonio, Texas

— 67 —

(65)

Ben Hecht and Morgenthauistic Racism

2615 W. Craig, San Antonio 1, Texas
January 4, 1947

Progressive
Madison, Wisconsin
To the Editor:

There are few people in the world with whom I find myself so often in agreement as with Milton Mayer. He helps me mightily to keep a small taper burning in my heart for the human race which Dean Swift's Brobdingnag called a "pernicious race of odious little vermin." Ben Hecht, whose play let's-rob-lie-kill-to-get-Palestine Mr. Mayer criticizes (January 6), keeps providing evidence that if the human race is one of odious little vermin, Ben Hecht is a particularly verminous specimen.

In a 1944 book, Ben Hecht let loose against all Germans as follows: "I am not interested in the Germans as musicians or scientists because you do not have to be a German to be either. To be a murderer, bold and gleeful, you have to be a German . . . I read in the fatness of their necks the mark of the murderer. I read in their watery eyes, their faded skins, their legs without feet, and their thick jaws, the fulfillment of a crime and the promise of another."

Sometimes one thinks that fellows like Hecht, Morgenthau, Baruch, Ludwig, and Winchell are determined to convince all Germans—including Americans who were born in Germany like Generals Krueger, Wedemeyer, and Willoughby (Tscheppe-Weidenbach)—that Hitler was right.

How grateful one is for the few brave voices like Milton Mayer's George Sokolsky's, David Lawrence's who prove by their decency and justice that among all races and among Christians and Jews however verminous, there are always at least some glowworms!

Sincerely,

Austin J. App, Ph.D.
Incarnate Word College
San Antonio 2, Texas

————————●●————————

(66)

Victors Starving the German People

2615 W. Craig Pl., San Antonio 1, Texas
February 25, 1947

The Christian Century
440 South Dearborn
Chicago, Ill.

Dear Mr. Morrison:

I want to thank you for your review of my book, **History's Most Terrifying Peace**, in your issue of February 12.

It struck me as an eminently fair review. Your reservations and criticisms were such which a thinking, dispassionate critic well might make. Had I had more space I would probably have added the things which would have satisfied the reservations.

I was especially pleased that you saw my underlying theme, which was not to attack Russia or to depict Russian atrocities for their own sake, but to suggest that the American policy of unconditional surrender made these crimes and injustices a foregone conclusion and that not only our govern-

— 68 —

ment but many of our church leaders of all denominations share a grave responsibility in what's wrong with the peace because of their inexcusable acceptance of a peace by unconditional surrender and dictation.

In that connection Barth's article in the same issue hits exactly the points which the peace dictators must hear and heed. We forced abject and total surrender on the German people—now its up to us to show that we can govern them better for their own and the world's good than they could have done themselves. A diet of 1500 calories, expulsions, territorial despoliation, industrial dismantlings can only prove that if Hitler was bad, the holy conquerors are worse.

I continue to admire the Christian Century for its consistent stand for a just peace and decent world order.

Sincerely yours,

Austin J. App, Ph.D.
Incarnate Word College
San Antonio 2, Texas

(67)

En-forced De-Nazification is a Crime

Mr. William Henry Chamberlin
Care of *New Leader*

Dear Mr. Chamberlin:
In July 1944 I met you at Antioch. Since then I have followed your writings with keen appreciation. Were all our writers as honest, as logical, and as well informed, lend-lease, Pearl Harbor, Unconditional Surrender, Morgenthauism, and the present world misery and mess would not have been.

My present remark, therefore, is not a criticism, only a comment or suggestion. In the *New Leader* for October 25 you say correctly, "Fortunately, the whole temper of modern society is such that a revival of persecution for religious faith in the western world seems to me unthinkable."

Specifically, as you word it, you are right. Yet this type of persecution has merely shifted its ground. Today, instead of an inquisition for one's theology, we have instituted an inquisition for one's political ideology. Americans and Britons and Russians are keeping tens of thousands of human beings in concentration camps because of the color of their political beliefs, and they have executed thousands of them for it. To me it seems incomprehensible that Americans who keep blathering about freedom of thought should have allowed themselves to be revenge-mongered into one of the worst and silliest thought-persecutions in history. Our whole policy of enforced De-Nazification is a crime. And every time we gave as a war motive the destruction of national socialism we declared that we believe in killing human beings because of their political ideology. To make war against a nation because of its form of government or its political ideas is the same thing as to make war against people on account of their religion —and it is as great a crime. It happens to be America's unique contribution to the long chain of man's stupidities and thought persecutions.

Sincerely yours,

Austin J. App, Ph.D.

Wars Fought by all Nations, not only Germans

1502 W. Ashby, San Antonio 1, Texas
January 4, 1948

Editor, *Fortune,*
350 Fifth Ave.
New York, N.Y.

Your December article, "Let Europe Consider the Swiss," while generally splendid and also fair to the Swiss, nevertheless displayed the collossal and insidious heresies about the Germans which Americans must educate themselves out of if they wish to help construct a just peace in Europe.

He asks why the Germans cannot like the teutonic Swiss get away from being "doomed to rule or be ruled, butcher or be butchered"? Who says they have been so doomed? Scholars and honest men do not.

In the world's most scholarly work on war, Quincy Wright's, Dr. Wright finds that "Of the 278 wars involving European states during this period (1480-1940), the percentage of participation by the principal states was: England, 28; France, 26; Spain, 23; Russia, 22; Austria, 19; Turkey 15; Poland, 11;. . . Germany (Prussia), 8; Italy (Savoy-Sardinia), 9. . ." (Volume I, p. 221). "The United States," he writes, "which has, perhaps somewhat unjustifiably, prided itself on its peacefulness, has had only twenty years during its entire history when its army or navy has not been in active operation during some days, somewhere" (p. 236).

Dorothy Thompson wrote that the attribution of sole guilt to Germany for World War I has been blown sky high by responsible historians who hold that "responsibility for the war was pretty generally distributed" (*Foreign Affairs,* July, 1935).

Nevertheless, the Germany smearers keep screaming that everybody must have a big army only the "warlike" Germans must remain unarmed in the middle of Europe—and let their women be raped by our lend-lease pals, the Russians. Take Boston away from the Americans, or Basle from the Swiss, and see how both would fight. Take Danzig from the Germans, and what can you expect?

Sincerely,

Austin J. App, Ph.D.

France Starving German POW's

1502 W. Ashby, San Antonio 1, Texas
January 18, 1948

Washington *Star*
Washington, D.C.

To the Editor:

According to an Associated Press report of January 17, "France received $53,000,000 worth of goods from the United States in the first 24 days after Congress approved interim aid to Europe," including 1,250,000 tons of coal, and 200,000 tons of petroleum.

In the meanwhile a CTPS report from Paris, dated December 29, declares that France has refused to liberate "German prisoners of war captured by the American Army and turned over to France" before 1949, "nearly four years after the end of the war." According to a New York Times report France still holds 600,000 of these unfortunate young men.

The Geneva International Red Cross has just protested to all the Allied Governments that so prolonging the captivity of German prisoners of war "cannot be justified. . . Prisoners are being held for labor and they thus are being kept for work because they are nationals of a country obligated to pay reparations." In other words the Four-Freedoms crusaders are using German prisoners of war as slave laborers.

Is it too much to ask that before our government sends any more billions to France, any more petroleum and coal, France liberate its 600,000 German prisoners of war, which we captured for them. Former Secretary of State Byrnes writes, **"I still believe that we should have insisted that France return the prisoners for whom we are responsible by October 1, 1947"** (SPEAKING FRANKLY, p. 169). Even 1947 is shamefully too late by two years!

But better later than still later. For the sake of Christian decency, badly bleeding, let us say to France, "The United States will no longer give handouts to nations that slave-labor prisoners of war."

Sincerely,

Austin J. App, Ph.D.
Professor, Incarnate Word College
San Antonio, Texas

———— ▪◦▪ ————

(70)

Re-educating the Vanquished by Force

1502 W. Ashby, San Antonio 1, Texas
February 7, 1948

The Tablet
1 Hanson Place
Brooklyn, New York

To the Editor:

I hope you will find space to print this letter in which I am giving three reverential cheers for Cardinal Michael Faulhaber, of Munich, Germany, for saying to the "holy" American Re-educators of Germany what I have been aching to hear some American Cardinal say to them.

What Cardinal Faulhaber told our self-appointed AMG re-educators of the Christian German people, according to a Munich report, was that "Many directives of the AMG. . . constitute an interference with internal German affairs. He contends it is a violation of natural law if the occupational power seeks the imposition of an educational system upon a conquered country." (N.C.W.C., Radio World, Feb. 1948).

All one can say to that is a long and fervent "Amen."

But, oh what a pity, that it wasn't an American cardinal who said it, that it wasn't all the American hierarchy together who said it, said it so loud and so strong that all Catholic priests, and editors, and professors, and the laity would have echoed and re-echoed it—so that the most nauseating of all holier-and-better-than-thou American might-makes-right presumptions, that of **re-educating** the seventy million German Catholics and Lutherans would have stuck in the throat of those who have been proposing it and choked them!

Let me repeat, we Americans have no business "re-educating" the Germans or the Japanese by right of our victory. One may not educate any people at the point of a bayonet. That our hierarchy did not immediate-

— 71 —

ly and definitely scotch this atrocious American policy of **enforced re-
education** of the conquered just proves again how war and nationalism
can blind even the spiritual leaders of even a so-called great democracy!
But I am glad that at least a conquered cardinal saw that might does not
give the right to club political ideology or religious ideology into people's
heads—and said so.

Sincerely,

Austin J. App, Ph.D.
Professor, Incarnate Word College
San Antonio, Texas

(71)

Gideonse on Prof. Beard's Rooseveltian Interventionism

1502 W. Ashby, San Antonio 1, Texas
June 16, 1948

The New Leader
7 East 15th Street
New York 3, N.Y.
Dear Sir:

In his quibbling review of Charles A. Beard's book on **President Roosevelt and the Coming of the War,** Harry D. Gideonse appears to ignore the
main thesis of Beard's book. That thesis is that Roosevelt while professing to the world and to the American people that he was trying to keep
America out of the war was in fact trying to push the country into the
war by every conceivable provocation, trickery, and swindle, even to the
point of violating the Constitution.

That is the point of the book—and that point is established beyond the
point of quibble.

If Mr. Gideonse lives by the Christian ethic that the end does not justify the means, then he must see that Beard's book constitutes a moral indictment of the President and his fellow interventionists that no outcome
could have justified, even if it had not been the horrible one of "history's
most terrifying peace," with a million women raped, fifteen million people
expelled from and robbed of their homes, five million known to have been
starved, millions of prisoners of war abused as slave laborers, half of
Europe destroyed, and ancient territories dismembered and stolen.

If Mr. Gideonse as a minimum at least believes in democracy, that
Beard's point ought to make him recoil in horror at the fact that in the
most important decision democratic America ever had to face its President
did not trust the people for their judgment but lied and swindled to them
while he underhandedly and dictatorially made and enforced the decision
himself.

Sincerely yours,

Austin J. App, Ph.D.

(72)

Anti-Semitism and Feeding Germans Arsenic

1502 W. Ashby, San Antonio 1, Texas
June 22, 1948

Editor, *American Mercury*
570 Lexington Ave.
New York 29, N.Y.
Sir:

I read with great interest Richard Hanser's article, "German Anti-

Semitism Today," and Erik V. Kuehnelt-Leddihn's reply in the June issue of the *Mercury*. Others besides Mr. Hanser remark a resurgence of Anti-Semitism in Germany, as polls also note it in the United States. (See *Fortune*, Oct., 1947). For that reason I wish Mr. Kuehnelt-Leddhin had tried to explain it rather than try to minimize it.

A **Race Relations** report (Dec.-Jan., 1947-48, p. 92) recommends "a far-reaching U.S. government-sponsored program of German re-education" to eradicate it.

I wonder whether it is possible to educate Germans out of anti-Semitism while important Jewish publicists go about saying that starving Germans should be fed arsenic. When the Bavarians protested by strike the starvation rations, Walter Winchell sneered, "Let 'em eat arsenic" (*Mirror*, Jan. 28, 1948).

The American Jewish Congress meeting in Boston, as reported by the Boston *Post* (Dec. 22, 1947), passed a resolution opposing "German Aid," and one Rabbi said that German children who were not starved after the First World War became paratroopers in the Second, which was the equivalent of Swift's "Modest Proposal" for the present starving children of Germany, only that Swift was ironic and this is a serious if sly suggestion to let German babies starve!

Over and above all this stands the America-sponsored peace policy, which when it was first introduced was denounced by our Secretary of State Hull as envisaging the extermination of thirty million Germans, and this plan is the Morgenthau Plan, fathered by a Jew whose name it bears, and never anything but supported by organized Jewry.

I wonder therefore ,whether to check anti-Semitism in Germany, it is not more important to re-educate the majority of the Jews away from eye-for-an-eye-ism into the Christianized attitude that characterizes a handful of Jews such as Victor Gollancz in England and five in this country, rather than start spending more government millions, not feeding the starving Germans but telling them not to dislike that branch of Semites which wants to feed them arsenic!

Sincerely yours,

Austin J. App, Ph.D.

———————◆◆———————

(73)

Governor Dewey and a Nasty Slur

1502 W. Ashby, San Antonio 1, Texas
June 30, 1948

Mr. Hamilton Fish
132 Nassau Street
New York 7, N.Y.

Dear Mr. Fish:

My writing you, with the intent of giving advice, is a presumption. But it is a presumption that springs from sincere regard, great admiration, and an urgent desire to see you regain your rightful place among the statesmen and politicians of the country. When you write or say anything which unnecessarily hurts those chances I feel like correcting you.

I was happy that you came out for Senator Robert Taft in TODAY'S WORLD as the most deserving Republican prospect. You were right. Senator Taft was the one candidate who is a man of principle more than of expediency.

But among the human race the most deserving seldom wins—he more often ends on the cross. It is therefore very important that when the world is full of utter scoundrels, some of whom are usually the powers behind the crucifixion of really good men, one does not drive an imperfect man, who is nevertheless still more on the side of lightness than darkness, into the arms of the evil by too harsh criticism or renunciation.

When Governor Dewey some years ago called you anti-Semitic for making the factual prediction that the New York Jews would vote for Roosevelt he did a grievous wrong; he did you an injustice, it is true, and he did it to appease the very people who had achieved your downfall. Of course he ought to have been brave enough to defy the evil forces. In any case he had no right, whatever the stakes, to slander you. Nevertheless, in the catalog of the world's crimes, his was not a major one. And a careful analysis of it leads to the suggestion that he did it more from the fear of being smeared and defeated as you were by the same forces that did it to you, that he did you wrong, not because he disliked **you**, but because he feared **them.**

Now, it is not inconceivable that a man whom a smear terror pushes into doing a wrong will feel secretly guilty towards the one wronged and perhaps anxious unobtrusively to make amends, and will feel resentful towards those who terrified him into the slander and perhaps determined to destroy that smear power once he is in a position to do so.

In any case, surely, you yourself consider Mr. Dewey almost angelic as compared to someone like Winchell. Therefore, it would seem to me very unwise to say things against Dewey which can only please and help people like Winchell, who in any case will never favor you, whatever you say, provided you are basically decent.

I am sorry you attacked Mr. Dewey so harshly. In one point I think your attack was particularly unfortunate—in the matter of his not having been in the armed service. If Mr. Dewey had whooped it up for intervention, and then evaded front line service, I would support your case. But Mr. Dewey was like you and me and Lindbergh and most far-seeing people a non-interventionist. Under those circumstances one may suppose that he considered our intervention of doubtful ethics. In that case, far from deserving blame for not volunteering, he might deserve praise. At any rate he did not need to make a martyr out of himself for a war he did not believe in—and if he was wise, could not believe in. I wish somehow you could undo some of the sting of that attack of yours. I wish you could make your peace with the Republican leadership—and again become influential among them. I want you in there. Men like you and Lindbergh have too many smear terrorists as enemies to be able to afford to attack people who are a little less fine than you but who are still not identifiable with the smear pack.

Sincerely yours,

Austin J. App, Ph.D.

————◆●◆————

(74)

Ilse Koch and the Alleged Lampshade

444 E. Tulpehocken, Phila. 44, Pa.
October 9, 1948

Inquirer
Philadelphia, Pa.
To the Editor of the Inquirer:

According to articles and letters in *The Inquirer* many people are whining for the skin of Ilse Koch and working themselves into ulcers because her sentence is for only four years. Some justify their lust for her skin because of the unproved allegation that lampshades of human skin were found in Buchenwald.

It is well to remind those who think so that, among similar things, one American soldier sent Roosevelt a letter opener which he had fashioned out of a Japanese skull. Though Roosevelt declined the "gift," the question for those who want to execute Ilse Koch for alleged and unproven association with human lampshades is whether this American who, not allegedly but certainly proudly, fashioned letter openers from human bones has been given more than the four years given to Ilse Koch. It is America's business to sweep the dirt from its own doors first. God will not blame America for being easy on Ilse Koch, but He will blame America for hanging and calumniating the members of other nations for deeds which it passes off as exuberance or souvenir hunting in its own Americans. Only after the American who made letter openers of Japanese bones has been punished have we any business worrying about Ilse Koch's crimes at all. If we don't want to hang him for his proven bone work then we have no business trying to hang Ilse Koch for her **alleged** lampshades.

For those who think Ilse Koch should be hanged because she was brutal to inmates, let them again first see whether all Americans have been hanged who were brutal in a similar fashion. Your October 8 issue carries the charge by President Judge E. Leroy van Roden, after he reviewed the Dachau war trials, that "Defendants . . . were badly beaten . . . Often the hoods placed over the prisoners' heads would be bloody from the beatings given other prisoners . . . Some investigators tried to get confessions by dressing themselves as priests." Are those who cry for Ilse Koch's skin working to see that these fellows get more than the four years given her? If not, then that is their first job. Among decent people, the dirt before one's own door gets priority!

Sincerely yours,

Austin J. App, Ph.D.

————————•◆•————————

(75)

Abuse of Germans Accused of Crimes

444 E. Tulpehocken, Phila. 44, Pa.
October 13, 1948

Washington *Star*
Washington, D.C.

To the Editor:

When in your October 2 edition you published Leon B. Poullada's letter describing the dubious methods and procedures of the so-called war crimes trials you did a great service to the American people which is painfully beginning to shake off the swamps of lies ten years of war propaganda has bogged them down in.

Confirming Mr. Poullada's courageous description are the disclosures of Judge E. Leroy van Roden, a member of the two-man commission reviewing the Dachau war crimes trials. Among other things he charges that "Defendants were kept in solitary confinement . . . many were badly beaten . . . investigators, dressed in Army uniforms, would conduct mock trials and sentence them to death . . . Often the hoods placed over the prisoners' heads would be bloody from the beatings given other prisoners.

— 75 —

Some investigators tried to get confessions by dressing themselves as priests" (*Philadelphia Inquirer*, October 9, 1948).

But you really hit the nail on the head—and suggested the only honest approach to this whole matter of the Taft-condemned war crimes trials—in your editorial of September 19. There you write what should be trumpeted into the ears of all the victors. Here it is:

"But before we get ourselves worked up over reducing from life imprisonment to four years the sentence imposed on the miserable wife of one slave master at Buchenwald we should ask ourselves whether it is equal justice under law (the law newly made at the war criminal trials) to condone by our silence the continued operation of Buchenwald under a new tribe of commandants" for under one of the victors and fellow trialist, the Russians, "the horror camp at Buchenwald is still operating at full tilt."

Sincerely yours,

Austin J. App, Ph.D.

----

(76)

Anti-Morgenthau Arguments Dewey Feared to Use

444 E. Tulpehocken, Phila. 44, Pa.
November 7, 1948

Brooklyn *Tablet*
1 Hanson Place,
Brooklyn, New York

To the Editor:

In your editorial on the election results (November 6), you rightly said that President Truman employed "flesh and blood arguments," but that Mr. Dewey employed "vague, platitudinous and over-the-head terms, such as unity."

That is true. But the tragedy of this election (and of the previous one) is that the Republicans again avoided the only issue in which the Democrats were shriekingly wrong and which ethics and justice absolutely required to be brought out, that is, that the Democrats lied us into the war ostensibly to achieve an Atlantic Charter peace, and then criminally lost the peace by exchanging Atlantic Charterism for Morgenthauism.

That the peace was lost, that New Deal unconditional surrenderism and Morgenthauism lost it, that government policies towards especially the vanquished are still reeking of injustices,—of dismantlings, of expulsions, of territorial robberies—that was the one ethically mandatory issue of the election—and that issue Mr. Dewey evaded for the second time in an escapist me-too-ism and by-partisanism.

To support one's country's foreign policy when it is unjust is a crime, not a virtue. Mr. Truman at Potsdam signed an edict, along with Stalin and Attlee, expelling millions of human beings from homes they occupied since before Columbus discovered America. At Nuremburg Americans hanged Germans for expelling some thousands of people. Yet this fearful Truman-supported expulsionism, which one bishop called "the greatest crime of the age," was not even mentioned by Mr. Dewey. So with other Morgenthauisms which played right into Russia's hands and which, with or without Russia, lost the peace—and had to lose the peace.

I am sorry Mr. Dewey lost—but I am more distressed that he did not say anything for which he deserved to win.

Sincerely yours,

Austin J. App, Ph.D.

(77)
Polish Oder-Neisse Prejudice

444 E. Tulpehocken, Phila. 44, Pa.
November 23, 1948

The Star
Washington, D.C.
To the Editor of The Star:

On October 14 you stated editorially that Russia and Poland "seized Germany's Eastern provinces" and "expelled many millions of Germans to the shrunken Reich." On October 27, Stefan Rogozinsky, Counselor to the Polish Embassy, defended these territorial seizures and expulsions.

Since Poland was predominantly Catholic, I hope you can print two Catholic items on the subject. One is that on March 1, Pope Pius XII, in a letter to the German bishops, referring to these expulsions, complaining asked, "Could anybody justify the expulsion of twelve million human beings from home and land to expose them to misery?"

The other is a resolution entitled, "American-Polish Stand on Eastern Germany," adopted at the 49th Annual Convention of the Catholic State League of Texas, affiliate of the Catholic Central Union, often called the oldest social justice organization in America. The Resolution as published in the October issue of *The Catholic Layman,* San Antonio, Texas, the League's official organ, reads as follows:

> "With a heavy heart every Catholic of whatever nationality has watched the many wrongs and tragedies Poland has suffered throughout the centuries. But a still sadder and greater tragedy would develop if Poland, seduced by communistic Russia, should destroy the sympathy of the right-thinking world by a territorial policy violating the pledged principles of the Atlantic Charter. This Charter, signed by all the United Nations, including Poland, declared specifically and unmistakably that 'no territorial changes' be made 'that do not accord with the freely expressed wishes of the people concerned.'

> "This principle did not justify territorial changes on the basis of historical or even economic argument. On November 16, 1944, the Catholic bishops collectively declared, 'We have no confidence in a peace which does not carry into effect, without reservations or equivocations, the principles of the Atlantic Charter.'

> "It is, therefore, of the utmost importance, first of all, to increase the Church's efforts in behalf of a just peace, secondly, to secure the sympathy of the world for Poland, that Americans of Polish extraction will be big and noble enough to apply the territorial principle of the Atlantic Charter in the matter of Germany's Eastern provinces now claimed by the communistic government of Poland.

> "Whatever their sentiments, based on old fatherland and historical grounds, may be, they must declare to their relatives in Poland, to the Germans, and to our government, that the western boundaries of Poland will strictly and honorably be drawn along the lines which honest plebiscites conducted before the expulsions indicated. Not only the honor of all Poles demands this, but the honor of American Catholics in general requires this policy of justice."

Sincerely yours,

Austin J. App, Ph.D.

---

(78)
When is a Jew a German

444 E. Tulpehocken, Phila. 44, Pa.
May 17, 1949

The Philadelphia *Inquirer*
Philadelphia, Pa.
To the Editor:

Your May 27 issue carried a sparkling item by Ollie Crawford, entitled, "British Lower the Curtain on the Eisler Melodrama."

— 77 —

It is perfect except for the second-last line, which contains a mistake in fact. The statement there is, "A German alien, Eisler, is charged with contempt of Congress."

This should read, "A Jewish alien, Eisler" etc. I hope you will print this letter as a correction.

UNRRA and IRO, as you know, distinguished carefully between Germans and Jews. Under these Eisler would have been entitled to relief and special considerations because he is a Jew, whereas "Persons of German ethnic origin, whether German nationals or members of German minorities in other countries" were excluded. (See Part II, Section 4 of the "Constitution of the International Refugee Organization.")

Common fairness, therefore, would seem to dictate that there be consistency all along the line—and honesty. Just as it would be wrong to call Ilse Koch a Jewess, so it is equally wrong to call Gearhart Eisler a German. If races and nationalities want to take credit for their Goethes and Einsteins, then it would not seem to be fair of them to try to push their Himmlers and Karl Marxes off on someone else.

Sincerely yours,

Austin J. App, Ph.D.

---

(79)

Msgr. Beran and the Czech Expulsion Crime

Hotel Furstenhof, Wien VII, Austria
July 8, 1949

The Tablet
128 Sloane St., S.W 1
London, England

To the Editor:
I want to compliment you on your article of June 25, entitled, "The Case of Monsignor Beran."

One footnote, however, is suggested to it. I just read in an Austrian paper for expellees, the sixteen million people of German ethnic origin thrown out of Eastern Germany, Sudetenland, and the Balkans, the following sentence:

> "The pot the Czechs have brewed for themselves, they now have to lap up!" We, the totally robbed and expelled Germans watch the climax with interest."

It is sad that when on June 23, 1945, the expulsion of the three million Sudetens began, Msgr. Beran sanctioned it as "an imperative necessity." Even the expulsion and confiscation of monasteries and nunneries owned by Sudeten monks and nuns were sanctioned.

This expulsion was an enormous, unequivocal crime committed while Czechoslovakia was still "free." Had Msgr. Beran and the Czech Catholics taken their stand then against that crime, they might never have been pushed against the present wall. Nor have people much of a case when their monasteries are confiscated if previously they sanctioned the confiscation of monasteries belonging to a group of co-religionst's whose language they disliked. It is a case of chickens coming home to roost—with a vengeance.

Sincerely yours,

Austin J. App, Ph.D.
Professor, La Salle College, Phila., Pa.

The Six Million — We Want Proof

Hotel Furstenhof, Wien VII, Austria
July 16, 1949

Miss Matilda Kazda (For the Editors)

Time
Rockefeller Center
New York 20, N.Y.

To the Editors:

I want to thank you sincerely for your letter of May 23 in which you cite the testimony of Dr. Wilhelm Hoettl given Nov. 26, 1945, to substantiate *Time's* statement which I had questioned, that six million Jews were "murdered" by the Hitler regime.

What was especially gratifying to me was that your letter tended to show that the Time editors actually believed that so many Jews were killed and were not, as I had suspected, merely repeating that old charge in order to please the Morgenthauists.

Nevertheless, I beg *Time* again, as I did a year ago, once and for all to make a thorough investigation of this problem. It is important to establish the facts, because now, everytime anyone demands an Atlantic Charter (just) peace for Germany, he is met with the sneer, "What did you do to prevent the murder of six million Jews by Hitler?" Recently when Catholic prelates protested the expulsion of Arabs from Palestine by the Zionists, that was the Zionist answer.

Clearly, a crime is a crime whether committed against one or against six millions. But quantity does matter, too. If Hitler in 1936 had for example totally robbed and ruthlessly expelled the 700,000 Jews in Germany and allowed 20 per cent of them to be abused to death on the way, it would have been a horrible crime, but it would not have been as vast a crime as the Czech expulsion of three million Sudetens, sanctioned in the Potsdam agreement, and the estimated abuse to death of 600,000 of these Sudetens.* Both fact and numbers are important in discussing atrocities.

When I came to Europe in June I had calculated from the best sources then available to me that about 1,500,000 Jews had lost their lives through the Nazis, some because they were partisans and spies, killed as America did or would have killed persons guilty of similar offenses.

After being here a month, evidences are accumulating that even that estimate is too high. I beg *Time* again to investigate the matter thoroughly. Surely the fact that even you could quote no better authority than that of a frightened, hysterical "Obersturmbannfuehrer," testifying four years ago, must make you suspect that if his figures could have been substantiated those who repeat the charge in order to persecute Germans would long ago have done so.

But in any case, I do sincerely thank you for your detailed and honest letter.

Sincerely yours,

A. J. App, Ph.D.

---

* Note added Jan. 11. 1965: Honest and impartial research have reduced that figure to 240,000.

Why Loans to Tito But Not to Franco

444 E. Tulpehocken St., Phila. 44, Pa.
December 23, 1949

Time Magazine
Time and Life Building
9 Rockefeller Plaza
New York 20, N.Y.

According to your report of Dec. 26, 1949, Democratic Congressman Joseph Pfeifer suggested in Madrid that America's objection to Spain was that its ruler Franco is a dictator, and his committee staff member, C. N. Marshall said, "We give loans only to governments who represent their people. Franco does not. Change your regime and we will change our policy toward you."

Mr. Pfeifer and Mr. C. N. Marshall could not have been alert when they said that. If what they imply and say were true, then America's lend-lease to Russia during the war would not have been given. More recently, the loan to Tito's Yugoslavia could not have been made.

In truth the New Deal government has found itself easily capable of making loans to dictatorial governments—provided the regimes were not only dictatorial but also atheistic, communistic, and anti-Christian.

Sincerely yours,

A. J. App, Ph.D.
Assoc. Prof. of English
LaSalle College, Philadelphia, Pa.

Copies to Congressman Pfeifer, and to **Arriba**.

Anti-Semitism and Anti-Germanism

444 E. Tulpehocken St., Phila. 44, Pa.
March 1, 1950

The American Legion Magazine
1 Park Ave.
New York 16, N.Y.

Gentlemen:

Though your article by H. Melchior and Will Sparks "What the Germans Really Think," (February, 1950), written by two "brotherhood boys" who do not yet know that anti-Germanism is just as reprehensible as anti-Semitism, was intended to continue the disgraceful Morgenthauism against Germany, it should arouse admiration for Germans in all readers who are honest and decent.

It proves that the Germans are more or less, exclusive of our Morgenthauists and other communistic scum, just like us Americans. Would we Americans like to see our country occupied by foreign soldiery, many of them thieving louts? Only the above-mentioned Morganthau and communist scum would, the same who want the Germans to want foreign occupation. Honest Americans want America clear and clean of any foreign occupation. So do the Germans. I was happy to note that in that article.

Any American who would want America occupied by foreigners is a traitor; any German who wants Germany occupied by a foregn army is a traitor too; any American who thinks Germans should want their country occupied by a foreign army is a communist, a Morgenthauist, or some other potential traitor.

Furthermore, the next time you get a parcel of Morganthauists to write an anti-German article for you, insist at least that they be not liars. That joke about rebuilding Germany in one year after forty is an American invention. I myself told it in Germany as an American joke—and no German had told it. But I certainly would not blame any German for telling it—it's a good joke, and has enough truth in it to deserve to be told.

But the definite lie in the article is the remark that the Adolf Bleibtreu letter in Munich caused an "anti-Jewish riot." That is a lie. I happened to have been in Bavaria at the time. What that letter created was an anti-German riot by the eye-for-an-eye boys who believe in freedom of the press for everybody except when it mentions them. The author of the letter has by the way not been found. It is very probable—I have proof of this having happened in another case—that it was written by Jews precisely to give them an excuse to start an anti-German riot. I don't say that the Bleibtreu letter was that—but there is some probability that it was. And I have proof of another instance where Jews wrote something flamingly anti-Jewish in order then to accuse the Germans of being anti-Semitic.

If you must have Morgenthauistic, prejudiced, and biased articles in your magazine, do at least insist that the scum who write them tell the factual truth. And try to remember that if anti-Semitism is wrong, anti-Germanism is just as wrong. If you don't know that yet, take a course in ethics and learn it. Remember too that nothing is wrong in Germans which would not also be wrong for us, and nothing is right for us which would not also be right for the Germans. Patriotism is the same sort of virtue everywhere. If you don't realize that you have no business editing a magazine for American veterans, of whom I am one.

Yours for more honesty and justice in the future,

A. J. App, Ph.D.

(83)

Answering Sneer Against Senators
Who Want Germans Treated Justly

444 E. Tulpehocken St., Phila. 44, Pa.
March 16, 1950

Editor, *Time* Magazine
9 Rockefeller Plaza
New York 20, N.Y.

To the Editor:

As expressed in your March 20 issue, "The Senate's Most Expendable," you do not like Senator William Langer of North Dakota, "Isolationist Langer", as you call him. But millions of Americans of German descent think of him as the Carl Schurz of the Twentieth Century. And other informed and just-thinking Americans esteem him for having seen in 1941, what everybody sees now, that the lend-lease bill would not stop totalitarianism but might put 800,000,000 million human wretches under it where in 1941 only 300,000,000 were under it. Millions admire him as one of the earliest and most consistent champions of a just peace for the vanquished in place of the infamous Morgenthau peace supported by senators you were careful not to ridicule!

His voice may be that of one, like St. John's, crying in the wilderness,

but his message and that of Senator Harry Pulliam Cain and William E.
Jenner will have to be multiplied and heard—or the Soviets will add to the
half of Europe and Asia the Morganthauists have already thrown into
their hands the rest of Europe and Asia. It is not so much selling atom
secrets to the Soviets that has given those beasts dominion over 800 million
people, but the warped and twisted revenge—and power politicians who,
instead of the Atlantic Charter, are dismantling German factories, are
slicing German and Japanese territories off to give to the Soviets and the
communist-ridden French, and ordered the expulsion of millions of Germans from their ancestral homes, and who now abuse Senator Pat McCarran for proposing legislation which would give these Expellees equal
rights with the so-called DP's.

Sincerely yours,

A. J. App, Ph.D.
Director, Boniface Press

(84)

The U. S. and the German National Anthem

444 E. Tulpehocken St., Phila. 44, Pa.
April 24, 1950

Phila. *Inquirer*
Phila., Pa.

To the Editor:

I am very glad that in your editorial of April 24 you clearly suggest
that for the Germans to sing "Deutschland ueber Alles" is nationalism, but
not Nazism. Nationalism is of course something we Americans are proud
of ourselves, and which therefore the Germans too should cultivate and be
proud of—at least if we seriously mean that we want to re-educate them
in our image!

The national anthem "Deutschland ueber Alles" is to Germany what
the "Star Spangled Banner" is to America. A German who is afraid or
who scorns to sing "Deutschland ueber Alles," or an American who is
afraid or who scorns to sing the "Star Spangled Banner" is a Hissling,
Quisling, or communist.

I was happy to see from your editorial that Dr. Konrad Adenauer, who
by force of occupation, is a puppet of the Western Allies, is not such a
Hissling, Quisling, or communist—but sings the German national anthem
as any decent American sings the American national anthem.

Sincerely yours,

A. J. App, Ph.D.

(85)

The Munich Pact Prevented War, Danzig Provoked It

August 7, 1950

Tablet
1 Hanson Place
Brooklyn, N.Y.

To the Editors:

In his letter to the TABLET (Aug. 5, 1950), Mr. Robert E. Reordan,
in expressing admiration for Father Gillis along with some disagreement,

— 82 —

also speaks of "the pact of Munich, whose cowardly provisions made World War II a certainty."

It has long been customary to speak of the "shameful appeasement at Munich," and to compare it with the appeasements at Yalta and Potsdam, where not only whole countries were signed over to Stalin but where the total expulsion and robbery of the peoples living in some of the stolen territory was prepared.

Nevertheless, this comparison is false. At Yalta and Potsdam, our government handed over to Soviet Russia totally non-Russian territories and peoples, such as East Prussia, and Eastern Poland—in flagrant violation of both the Fourteen Points of Wilson and the Atlantic Charter of Churchill and Roosevelt.

The literal opposite occurred at the Munich Pact of September 29, 1938. This Pact, far from violating Wilson's Fourteen Points, was a belated and long-overdue adjustment according to it. Its main provision was that the Sudetenland, a territory the size of Maryland with 3,653,300 German inhabitants, was finally granted its self-determination wish of 1919, union with Germany and Austria. The Munich Pact was belated justice, not shameful appeasement. If it did not prevent the Second World War it was not because it revised the Versailles Treaty, but because it did not revise the Versailles Treaty everywhere. The "everywhere" was Danzig and the Corridor. The Danzigers, too, should then have finally been granted the Fourteen Points Guaranteed self-determination, that is, belated justice, not "shameful appeasement." Had this been done World War II might still have been averted. And in any case it could then not have sprung from the Versailles injustices of the Allies. The Munich Pact has nothing in common with the utterly unjustifiable sell-out of German, Finnish, Polish, and Japanese territories to the Soviets, of which our Administration has been guilty at Yalta and Potsdam and since.

Yours truly,

A. J. App, Ph.D.

------

(86)

The Catholic Church and the 'Holy War' on Communism

Open Letter to Peaceloving Protestants Who are Disturbed on This Point
Sept. 1, 1950

At a Friends' Institute for International Relations, held in Reading, Pa., this August, many of the participants were agitated by the following three convictions regarding Catholicism, namely, that the Catholic Church is implacably opposed to communism and Soviet Russia, that she is promoting a "Holy War" against Communistic Russia, and that the so-called Soviet-Russian problem is essentially nothing more than a struggle for power between **totalitarian** Soviet Russia on the one side and the **totalitarian** Roman Catholic Church on the other.

Since the late Rabbi Stephen S. Wise last year also accused the Church of being "uniquivocally for war" (Wash. *Star,* March 19, 1949) and Dean William Ralph Inge, of London's St. Paul's this month spoke of the Church as being a "totalitarian religion" (*Time,* Aug. 28, 1950), it may be assumed that many non-Catholics share these misconceptions and would welcome a clarifying comment.

It is true that the Catholic Church is unequivocally opposed to communism. On March 19, 1937, five days after he had in the Encyclical "Mit

Brennender Sorge" pointed out the errors of National Socialism, Pope Pius XI declared in his Encyclical "On Atheistic Communism":

"Communism is intrinsically wrong, and no one who would save Christian Civilization may collaborate with it in any undertaking whatsoever."

This was and is also the view of the Catholic hierarchy and laity, here and everywhere. The present Pope recently restated it. And it is surprising that people who applauded the Pope's condemnation of National Socialism do not similarly applaud his repudiation of communism!

But neither the Pope nor the hierarchy nor the majority of the laity want a "shooting" war against Soviet Russia. If one is honest one may not **except** only in a figurative sense speak of a "holy war" of the Church against communism. One may say so only in the sense in which St. Paul speaks of the "war" between the spirit and the flesh. Precisely now, when in America it has become virtually suspect to talk of "peace," when the big newspapers use it guardedly in quotation marks, it is notably the Pope who in his recent "Summi Maeroris" called "for public prayers for world peace," and diocesan Catholic papers carried the news often in large headlines, such as, "Church Always Detests War; Pray Against It, Pleads Pope Pius XII."

Thirdly, speaking of the Catholic Church as a "totalitarian" power engaged in a power conflict with totalitarian Soviet Russia rests on a pathetic confusion of moral force with political and physical force. A totalitarian state is one which orders and controls the political, economic, educational and social life of all its members and enforces its single party system with the gun and the concentration camp. But the Catholic Church has no guns and no concentration camps. It is **authoritarian,** not totalitarian. It prescribes for membership, which is **voluntary,** certain rules and the acceptance of certain beliefs or dogmas, and simply states that anyone who does not accept these is not or is no longer a member. That, and nothing more. She does not beat him into acceptance, she does not jail him, she does not even order him to leave any particular house of worship physically. Her power is only moral: she binds only the consciences of those men who voluntarily want to be so bound. She does not bind them physically. She employs no guns and no secret police.

Let anyone imagine Stalin's government using only such moral force, and no bayonets or tanks or concentration camps. And then let him ask himself whether it would be fair then to apply to such a Russia the same term "totalitarian" which the Interventionists applied to Nazi Germany.

And let no one confuse Franco with Catholicism, any more than Ben Gurion with Judaism and the King of Sweden with Lutheranism! No Catholic temporal ruler is the Church, and furthermore, in this imperfect world, Christians including churchmen must support many a ruler and many a government, many of whose policies, they do not and cannot support. No Churchmen could support the Morgenthau Plan, yet none of them advocated the overthrow of our government.

The three misconceptions here commented on are dangerous. In these times so critical for Christian civilization, there are enough problems even if people try heroically to be fair and wise. Christians, Protestant or Catholic, cannot afford to indulge in any misconceptions towards one another.

A. J. App, PhD.

World Jewish Congress and Vengeance

February 28, 1951

Inquirer
Philadelphia, Pa.

Dear Sir:

According to a report in your issue of February 28, The World Jewish Congress calls for the immediate blood of seven more Germans and protests the State Department's thirty-day reprieve to study an appeal.

In this connection it may interest your readers to learn that a Catholic priest of the Ruhr District in Germany, Rev. Augustin Flossdorf, "has offered to go to the gallows in place of any one of the German war criminals." Father Flossdorf had himself been confined at one time in Nazi concentration camp. Presumably he has risen high enough to slough off the eye-for-an-eye passions and to practice Christ's turning-the-other cheek culture.

But more important for us, he alleges that as long as Allied individuals have not been executed who committed war crimes, these Germans should not be executed either. Perhaps The World Jewish Congress might do well to ask themselves what they have done to get the murderers of Count Bernadotte executed as had been pledged by the Israeli authorities, but so far not done.

Sincerely yours,

A. J. App, Ph.D.

Hitler Right in Correcting Versailles Injustices

March 5, 1951

Freeman
240 Madison Ave.
New York 16, N.Y.

To the Editor:

I am happy that Ludwig von Mises in his review of Erich Eyck's Bismarck (Jan. 8, '51), considers it "a most valuable contribution."

Some questions, however. Mr. von Mises castigates Bismarck for hanging non-uniformed guerillas. Is not that standard practice, approved by international law? Aren't our generals doing this to such guerillas in Korea?

Mr. von Mises introduces as a horrible consequence of Bismarck's ideas Hitler's violating "step by step the essential clauses of the Treaty of Versailles." How should Hitler have broken them? All at once? Or by a burst of bombs?

Were not the clauses of the Versailles Treaty which Hitler broke unjust clauses? If they were, then it was the duty of every leader anywhere to break them as soon as possible. It was a pity that the world waited for Hitler to crack the Versailles Treaty. It should never have been made, but once made, it should have been our American statesmen who should have violated it "step by step." An atrocity must not be obeyed, it must be violated—to cooperate with injustice is a new injustice.

Let's blame Hitler for the things in which he was wrong, not for those in which he was right. There is enough ethical confusion in the world without adding more. When Hitler demanded the Sudetenland, and Dan-

zig, and the removal of the Versailles guilt clause and similar ones he was
right. The pity is, not that he made those demands, but that our American
statesmen did not forestall his demands.

Sincerely yours,

A. J. App, Ph.D.

(89)

IF U M T Right for U. S. it is also for Germany and Japan

March 13, 1951

Phila. *Inquirer*
Philadelphia, Pa.
To the Editor:

I agree so generally with your columnist, Ivan H. Peterman, that it is
almost a pleasure finally to report a difference of opinion. In the March 13
issue, complaining that "Congressmen Haggle Over A Vital Need," he
suggests that because Generals Marshall, Eisenhower, Bradley, Patton,
and Arnold want Universal Military Training, therefore Congress should
unhesitatingly adopt it.

As I see the unanimity of the generals in urging UMT should rather
arouse everybody's suspicion. They all plunked for UMT way back in
1944 and 1945. At that time they were all palsy-walsy with the Russians
and declared that once the Germans were forever de-militarized, there
would never again be war. And then they disarmed the Germans, blew
up all German defences, and forbade the Germans to have even as much
as military bands. Yet at the same time, they plunked for UMT!

They did not get it. Then somehow the Korean "police action" devel-
oped. And instead of clearing it up, the generals have spent their major
efforts using it as a club to force the American Congress into adopting the
same UMT they had urged in 1945.

If UMT was a crime in Germany when Hitler and his generals urged
it in 1935, then it is equally a wrong when American generals urged it in
1945, and urge it in 1951. If UMT is good, then it is good for everybody,
that means also for the Germans and the Japanese. If it is not good for
everybody, then it is not good or right for us. That is not the most intrinsic argument against it, but it is one which every American ought to
recognize easily. When a thing is really good, like religion, then we want
it for everybody!

Sincerely yours,

A. J. App, Ph.D.

(90)

The Vanquished Lose No Rights
But the Victors Lose their Honor

March 27, 1951

America
329 W. 108th Street
New York, N.Y.
To the Editor:

Clearing my desk during the vacation I came upon your editorial,
"Dangerous Demagogy" of your August 20, 1949 issue. That is far back,
but its implications are so important that I write this note anyhow.

Rebuking German politicians for their election demands, you say,

"Messrs. Schumacher and Adenauer might also reflect that the hateful
Americans are bound by nothing but charity to permit the German federal
republic to become a party" to FCA and to a relaxation of Allied controls
on German internal and international affairs.

I wonder whether on reflection you would not modify that statement
to read: "Whether the Germans have the power to demand it or not, the
Allies are bound, not only by vague charity but also by justice, as clearly
defined in the Atlantic Charter and by international law, to treat the Germans exactly as they interpret those principles for themselves and among
one another and in conformity with the divine mandate to treat others as
they wish to be treated themselves."

As I see it, since might does not make right, the Germans, even
though they lost the war, have exactly the same rights we Americans have
since they belong to the same unfortunate and usually vicious human race.
If that is true, then it is the duty of their politicians to demand these
rights. Am I right about this?

Sincerely yours,

A. J. App, Ph.D.

---

(91)
Morgenthauists Hate McCarthy, Jenner, Cain

April 12, 1953

Commonweal
386 Fourth Avenue
New York 16, N.Y.
Gentlemen:

Now that the heat of the election campaign is long over, and the
danger of being smeared reactionary, isolationist, fascist, or anti-Semitic
if one supported McCarthy-Taft-Eisenhower has somewhat subsided, too, I
timidly rise to make one comment on your Skillin-Cogley-O'Gara-Clancy
"Choice for President" statement of September 26, 1952.

In your support of Stevenson, your particular objection to Eisenhower
seems to have been some of the company on his side. After attacking
Senator John Bricker of Ohio, you further lash out as follows:

"The General would thus have performed an historic service to both his
country and his party by saving them from the threat of the McCarthys, the
Jenners, the Dirksens, and the Cains . . ."

In thus attacking McCarthy, Jenner, Dirksen, and Cain were you
aware that you were attacking just about the leading senators who when
it was unpopular to do so demanded a Christian, a just treatment of the
vanquished Germans? At that time many of the senators who stood with
Stevenson fought even against relief shipments for the German people. In
short they were vengeful baby-starvers at heart. What wrong even in
your eyes could McCarthy-Jenner-Dirksen-Cain have possibly committed
that was as vicious as that of the Morgenthauistic senators who, as even
Hull stated, would have exterminated half of the German race and delivered the remnants to Moscow had the senators you denounce along with
Taft, Langer, McCarran, Capehart not blunted the Morgenthau plan?

If the *Commonweal* really wants to be as impartial towards all races
and peoples as it proclaims then it should stop smearing precisely those
senators who are trying to correct the frightful injustices against the
German people in the Yalta and Potsdam pacts, the pacts that among other
crimes expelled fifteen million Germans from their ancient homelands, killing some three million men, women, and children in the process.

Yours truly,

A. J. App, Ph.D.

East Germany, Middle Germany, West Germany

March 27, 1955

Time Magazine
Time and Life Building
9 Rockefeller Plaza
New York 20, N.Y.
Dear Sir:

I was thrilled to note in your "Yalta Story" (March 28) that you deplored in the Yalta record "an almost total absence of the pursuit of justice" which you rightly call "the only enduring restraint upon power." As far as I saw, *Time* was the only publication that pointed up this all-consuming shortcoming of theYalta proceedings and Pact.

This satisfaction was somewhat dampened by your footnote calling the German designation of Oder-Neisse Germany as East Germany and the Soviet-occupied part of Germany as Middle Germany as "Patriotic German jargon for the Soviet zone." The word "jargon" has an evil connotation. Yet the Germans are literally correct in using those terms. In truth and justice the Soviet Zone is "Middle Germany" and the 44,231 square miles taken from Germany at Yalta in violation of the Atlantic Charter is "East Germany." Incidentally this temporarily lost Germany is larger than South Korea to maintain which America fought a war! This Oder-Neisse Germany is larger than all of Ireland (31,839 sq. Mi.) by an area twice the size of Israel (5,500 sq. mi.).

Aren't the Germans justified in referring to this one-fourth of prewar Germany as East Germany, the one-fourth occupied by the Soviets as Middle Germany? And does not the Atlantic Charter to which America in 1941 was pledged require us to help Germany regain those territories taken away from it at the unjust Yalta Conference?

Yours truly,

A. J. App, Ph.D.
La Salle College

Publicity, Not Merit, Determines 'Who's Who'

May 24, 1958

To the *Tablet*
Brooklyn, N.Y.
Dear Sir:

When in your recent item on "Who's Who" you show that some very important judges and doctors were nevertheless not dignified with inclusion in the American "Who's Who," you put the finger on a factor too little understood: popularity and recognition are not so much proportionate to merit as to publicity, often shrewdly managed publicity.

Many of the great reputations in American life and letters during the last 40 years are due to what Sheridan in *"The Critic"* called the art of puffing, and "Who's Who" includes those who have been everywhere most puffed up.

Most of those included, deserve inclusion, some don't, and decidedly many are not included simply because their character and ideas caused them in the present prevailing secular and collectivist atmosphere to be treated with as much silence as they can safely be given.

In my field of literature, the great reputations in our lifetime have depended more frequently on ideology, congeniality to the left, than to merit. A good case in point is the prestige vicissitude of novelist John Dos Passos. The Dos Possos who demonstrated for Communists Sacco-Vanzetti and shared a prison cell with Communist Michael Gold shared until 1945 equal honors in all anthologies of contemporary American literature with Faulkner and Hemingway.

Then when as a correspondent in Europe he saw the bestialities of the Soviets in Vienna and other cities, when at the Nuremberg trials he saw them try to pass their murder at Katyn of thousands of Polish officers off to the Germans, and then dared to say these things, his reputation abruptly dropped.

Forrest Davis, reviewing Dos Passos' latest novel, "The Great Days," dealing with the perception and consequent persecution of James Forrestal, speaks of "Dos Possos' decline from liberal-leftist favor once he had perceived that beyond the Nazi lay a further and even more formidable dragon which the West must slay to save itself" ("National Review," April 26, 1958, page 402).

Dos Passos is now virtually ignored in all texts and classroom anthologies. In a standard anthology for American literature courses, first edition, 1934, third edition, 1947, Hemingway had 17 pages, Wolfe, eight, Dos Possos, seven, Faulkner, six. But in a standard recent anthology, 1955, Hemingway has five pages, Wolfe, 22, Faulkner, seven—and Dos Passos has **none.** He is not even mentioned in the index!

It may be hard for the American public to realize that literary reputations rise or fall more by the favor of the prevailing critics than by intrinsic merits—and the prevailing critics have not smiled on anyone aggressively non-secular or anti-Communistic.

For the latter, if not altogether the silent treatment, there has more often been a sneer than a smile. This is probably true in all areas: it is certainly true in the literary. But "Who's Who" naturally is compiled from those enjoying the most smiles and the most coverage.

A. J. App, Ph.D.
Associate Professor of English,
LaSalle College, Phila., Pa.

(94)

Israeli Call Nasser "Fascist"

November 12, 1958

Inquirer
Philadelphia, Pa.

To the Editor:

Your Sunday edition carried an AP dispatch from Tel Aviv in which the Israeli Foreign Minister, Mrs. Golda Meir, calling Nasser "the Fascist dictator of Egypt," declared:

"We have said all along that Nasser is a threat to the world—that he is the man who will cause the third world war. But no one would listen. No one believed us."

In as much as it was the Israeli who made the surprise attack on Egypt, not the other way around, one is flabbergasted at Mrs. Meir's logic.

If Mussolini, after invading Ethiopia in October 3, 1935, had said, "We always said Emperor Haile Selassie is a threat to the world and is

the man who will start a second world war," he would have been given
the horse laugh!

I am glad the *Inquirer* has not tried to glorify the Israeli-British-
French aggression on Egypt.

Yours respectfully,

A. J. App, Ph.D.

---

(95)

U. S. Confiscates Alien Private Property

December 7, 1956

Newsweek
Broadway and 42nd Street
New York 36, N.Y.

To the Editor:

Henry Hazlitt's plea in "For the Rule of Law" (Dec. 10) for a return
to international respect for private property in peace and in war is well
taken. Certainly "an international Magna Charta" to protect "foreign
property and other foreigners' rights" is an urgency.

Mr. Hazlitt properly points out how many times in the last twenty
years the American Government has condoned the confiscation of foreign
property by some nations. What needs also to be pointed out is our Government's own reversion to lawless confiscation of private property.

On October 18 some of us asked the Secretary of State Dulles, happily
a man who does know right from wrong and prefers right, why the Government has not yet made restitution on the half billion dollars worth of
private German and Japanese property still illegally held confiscated. He
said that while he had always favored full return as a moral obligation,
he regretted to have to say the Government did not have the funds available to make full restitution at present!

How sad that our Government which has billions for foreign boon-
doggles, even billions for Communist Tito, does not have half a billion to
make restitution for the private property it stole from Germans and
Japanese!

Yours truly,

A. J. App, Ph.D.
Assoc. Prof. of English, LaSalle College

---

(96)

Dismantling Made Feeding Germany Necessary

December 30, 1956

The Wall Street Journal
44 Broad Street, New York

To the Editor:

In your editorial on the critical "Letter from Germany" by Herman
Baer from Hamburg you gently urge him to be more appreciative of America's feeding and supporting the Germans only "a very few years (after)
we were planning to reduce them to a pastoral state" (Dec. 28).

Since the *Wall Street Journal* blessedly from the start opposed this
genocidic pastoralization for several years after the war (dismemberment,
mass expulsions, dismantlings), I hope you won't mind my saying that
eventual American aid to Germany after the Morgenthauistic expulsions
and dismantlings can be likened to giving a family a prefabricated garage

— 90 —

after one savagely burns their house down and has let them sleep in a ditch several nights.

When Germany surrendered in 1945 it was still a going concern, more than able to feed itself. The victors destroyed its remaining facilities and factories and even poisoned the garbage of the occupying troops so that no German child might be kept from starvation by eating it! Our eventual aid was like throwing a cripple some gunny sacks after having torn his clothes off and left him shivering naked several nights. Our wanting appreciation for it is as if the Samaritan had fallen upon the merchant, lacerated him and robbed him of all his goods, and then after a few days returned with some salves and rags—and thereafter claimed a boy scout medal for his charity and generosity!

Of course the Germans should be grateful that America did not like the Soviets persist in the Morganthauism. But we Americans should remain ashamed to have adopted the Morgenthau pastoralization plan at all!

Respectfully,

A. J. App, Ph.D.

(97)

The Bridge: Jews Summoned, Not Destined

5353 Magnolia St., Phila. 44, Pa.
February 19, 1957

Brooklyn *Tablet*
1 Hanson Place
Brooklyn, New York

To the Editor:

To your sympathetic review of *The Bridge.* A Yearbook of Judaeo-Christian **Studies,** edited by Father John M. Oesterreicher ("himself a convert from Judaism") in your issue of February 16, a few sentences from Father Joseph Clifford Fenton's review in *The American Ecclesiastical Review* (January, 1957, pp. 68-72) might be helpfully added.

Father Fenton, after praising especially two articles ("The Word is a Seed," and "The Community of Qumran") says "the editor of *The Bridge* was less felicitous in his introduction to the present volume": when he speaks of the Jews being **destined** together with us to eternal salvation," he should instead have said that they are "**summoned** or **called** together with us to the same eternal salvation. There is a world of difference between the two formulae."

Saying *"The Bridge* seems somewhat remiss," this authoritative review continues:

> *"Its emphasis seems always on points of similarity between Judaism and Catholicism. It contains frequent and emphatic mention of injustices Jews have received at the hands of Christians, and, in general, speaks in such a way as to make the reader imagine that, after all, the Jew of New Testament times is in a fair position spiritually despite his rejection of and opposition to Our Divine Lord. It tends to cover up the need for repentance and Baptism, a need as urgent upon the Jew as it is upon any other man who has not as yet been incorporated into the Church by the sacrament of faith."* (p. 71)

Father Fenton calls "Father Journet's 'The Mysterious Destinies of Israel' the longest and by far the least satisfactory contribution to this volume of *The Bridge.*"

Respectfully,

A. J. App, Ph.D.

— 91 —

Father Gillis, Champion of Justice

April 3, 1957

Rev. John B. Sheerin, C.S.P.
Editor, *Catholic World*
411 W. 59th Street
New York 19, N.Y.

Dear Father Sheerin:

First of all I want to thank you for carrying my article, "Why Americans Succeed" in the April issue, so apt for the coming May 1 feast day of "St. Joseph the Worker" and for giving it the lead position. Especially was I delighted to see the wonderful picture above it. Virtually everyone at LaSalle who saw the article commented on the appropriateness and beauty of that picture—it impressed me with the knack good editors have of digging up suitable things.

When on March 15 I spoke at the Scholastic Press Conference at Columbia, the first New York paper I opened carried the news that Father Gillis had died! I was deeply moved. Personally, he had long been an editorial friend of mine, accepting what I believe many of the best articles I ever wrote. I had met him several times. Ideologically, as the years went by I felt him more and more to be like a prophet of old, a champion of international justice and political honesty, and as you so wonderfully put it in your excellent Sum and Substance article, "Guardian of Our Freedoms," a guardian of human liberty and Christian dignity. Many a time in the dark, unreasoning, Morgenthauistic days of the Yalta and Potsdam sell-outs I found him a beacon and a consolation and from his "Sursum Corda" articles took the courage in my own modest way to cry out against the shameful travesty of justice perpetrated by the "peacemakers" of the World War II carpetbag era.

For Father Gillis's uncompromising and trenchantly logical stand for liberty and justice in national and international affairs my profoundest thanks to the God of Right and Justice—and to the Paulists for producing him, and to the Catholic Press for giving him a platform!

May he rest in the peace he so richly deserves.

Sincerely yours,

A. J. App, Ph.D.

———————

What Even Handed Justice Means

April 3, 1957

Mr. Otto A. Sinkie
The Altruist
304 West 6th Street
Grand Island, Nebraska

Dear Mr. Sinkie:

Your effort to prevent a global war with nuclear weapons by trying to mobilize "the minds and hearts of the people for their own preservation from war to peace" is a noble one—and I gladly contribute my thoughts on "how to develop a frame of mind and an attitude of heart that will tend to insure world peace."

Wars come from fear of other nations; fear leads to power politics;

power politics lead to international injustices and it is these that lead to new wars.

John Foster Dulles, our Secretary of State, in a new preface to his book, *War and Peace,* originally published in 1950, writes now:

> *"Even as I write, there are grave injustices such as servitude of the Soviet satellites and the division of Germany, Korea, and Vietnam. . . Such injustices tend ultimately to lead to resort to force unless other means of change exist. . ."* (*Newsweek,* April 8, 1957).

What "other means of change" can be invoked? The American people and the people of all the world and their governments must put more trust in God so as to have less fear of any enemy; they must abandon power politics—the policy of opposing this or that nation, not because it is wrong, but because it is strong or getting stronger—and must practice a resolute justice to one and all other nations. They must stop, as Ruskin wrote, being "guided by balances of expediency," which is power politics, and be guided "by balances of justice."

God did not command any nation to become the strongest, He did not guarantee any nation security: He did command every nation to be just in its dealing with other nations and to trust Him for its security. With a proper trust in the goodness and justice of God nations would stop being afraid of any nation growing bigger than themselves. Trustful of God rather than fearful of rival nations, they would stop indulging in power politics, in unfair methods and evil-intentioned alliances to keep dynamic rivals down. They would then work harder at trying to be fair and just to rival nations than they work ringing them in with military bases, to block their access to certain raw materials, to hurt them by trade discriminations.

Soviet Russia was just as communistic and as evil in 1941 as it is in 1957. But in 1941 we showered it with lend-lease billions, whereas now we direct a cold war against it. Tito's Yugoslavia is just as communistic and just as evil as Soviet Russia, but Tito enjoys annually millions of American foreign aid. Why the difference? Only because Soviet Russia, after the destruction of German power, accomplished with American arms and Unconditional Surrenderism, has become the only nation that can rival America in military strength.

Because we treat Communistic Russia and Communistic Yugoslavia with balances of expediency instead of with balances of justice, flattering Yugoslavia and cold-warring Russia, even decent Russians have a right to suspect American motives and American honesty.

If on the other hand America would treat all nations, including its closest Allies with an even-handed justice; if it had uncompromisingly required of all of them policies in harmony with the Atlantic Charter; if in 1945 it had required France to give self-determination to Saar, and ordered the Czechs to give it to the Sudetens, and had itself given it to the Austrians (to stay with Germany if they wished), then America could now proudly and effectively tell Soviet Russia to give Hungary self-determination—and the other Balkan and the Baltic nations under Soviet rule. But it then could also require Soviet Russia to give self-determination to Middle-Germany, but again only if it would also require Poland unequivocally, to give self-determination with return to their homelands to all the Germans of the Oder-Neisse territories. More examples like that could be given.

Only if America would uncompromisingly, with friend and enemy, require adherence to the principles of the Atlantic Charter and would itself live up to them—as in making restitution of the half billion dollars private

German and Japanese property confiscated after the war—would America
seem honorable in its propaganda campaign against Soviet Russia. Only
then could America hope for a peaceful and just ending of the ten-year-old
cold war.

Yours truly,

A. J. App, Ph.D.

(100)

German Generals and "Krauts"

December 5, 1957

The *Inquirer*
400 N. Broad Street
Philadelphia, Pa.

To the Editor:

As one who was named in his column of December 2, I am surprised
that your columnist, Robert C. Ruark, born in old Confederate territory
(North Carolina), keeps sniping at the recently appointed NATO general,
Hans Speidel, as unqualified because the Germans lost the war.

Would he say that Robert E. Lee was an unqualified general because
the Confederacy lost its Civil War? The *Columbia Encyclopedia* speaks of
some general as "the greatest American general between Washington and
Lee," making the loser Lee one of the greatest! Recently the Civil War
Round Table of New York rated Confederate losers Lee, Stonewall Jackson and Nathan B. Forrest as among the eleven greatest generals of the
Civil War.

It ill behooves Ruark to keep insulting Speidel because his government
lost the war. Against the combined British, Soviet, and American em-
pires, does he think any general could have won? If not, then he should
stop letting his anti-German prejudices show. He should stop referring to
Speidel or the German people as "krauts." I am sure he would act out-
raged if any columnist called some other nationality by, for example, the
name that rhymes with "tike."

Once and for all, it is high time all columnists and publishers realized
that anti-Germanism is every bit as reprehensible as anti-Semitism. And
Ruark's implication that those who say so should go live in Germany is
about as nasty as a scribbler can get! I am sure a little thought will make
him realize that himself.

Yours respectfully,

A. J. App, Ph.D.

(101)

Distorting a Nazi Song

February 14, 1958

The *Bulletin*
Philadelphia 1, Pa.

To the Editor:

I want to express my appreciation of Holmes Alexander's interesting
article on why the German Scientists "dominate the Missile Field" (Feb.
13). His tribute to Von Braun and Dr. Struhlinger was perceptive and
justified, and his suggestion for improving our scientific work is worth
heeding.

With regard to his quoting "the boast of the Hitlerite Nazis . . .

— 94 —

"Today, we rule Germany—tomorrow, the world'," I should like to offer a comment. While the pertinent Nazi song is indeed often quoted that way, it should properly be translated: "Today, Germany will hear us—Tomorrow the whole world." The German words were: "Heute hört uns Deutschland—Morgen, die ganze Welt." It was easy for enemy propagandists to substitute "gehört" for "hört" and so produce a more aggressive meaning which could be used to promote American intervention.

Yours truly,

A. J. App, Ph.D.

---

(102)

The Inflated Figure of 6,000,000

July 1, 1959

The *Inquirer*
Philadelphia, Pa.
Letter to the Editor

Dear Sir:

That according to your UPI dispatch, Jerusalem, June 30, the Israeli foreign affairs committee, opposed viciously by the left-wing parties, favors selling grenade launchers to West Germany, the West's ally, is a good omen for eventual reconciliation between the German and Jewish peoples.

But this must be founded not only on charity, or on justice, but above all on truth. A serious obstacle is the continued, totally un-established charge, repeated in the UPI dispatch, "of the extermination of six million Jews in Nazi Germany."

These unproven, grossly inflated statistics offend not only every German by nationality or ethnic origin, but also every lover of historical accuracy. Certainly, for example, those who wish have a right to keep charging that the Israeli robbed 900,000 poor Arabs of their old homes in Palestine; but **no one** has a right to inflate this number to 5,400,000.

The Red-inspired statistics of six million, utterly unsubstantiated, benefits only the Reds. It is unworthy of honest Jews, and an insult to an age which prides itself on accuracy.

Yours truly,

A. J. App, Ph.D.

---

(103)

Discrepant Eichmann Quotes

June 1, 1960

Newsweek
444 Madison Avenue
New York 22, N.Y.

To the Editor:

In your "The Eichmann Trackdown," you state categorically that "Hitler officially decided in 1941 that all Jews were to be killed." Since even the Nuremberg investigations turned up no such extermination documents, I am wondering when the one you base yourself on turned up? Will you please quote it exactly, with reference?

Also, can you give exact reference for your quoting Eichmann as saying in 1945 that he will jump into his grave laughing because he had "six million lives" on his conscience? If your quote is statistically correct, then was the identical quote of *Time* (June 6) in error? *Time* writes

— 95 —

that a **witness reported** that Eichmann boasted in the exact words you give except that Eichmann is reported as having said, "I have 5,000,000 human beings on my conscience."

Is it five million, or six million? If Jews are as good as other people, then it seems to me journalists should not wantonly gas a million more or fewer—on their typewriter! If accuracy is a virtue in other matters, why not also in the matter of how many Jews were executed?

Yours for exact reporting,

A. J. App, Ph.D.
President, FACGD

Copy to *Time*

—————————•♦•—————————

(104)

No One Gassed at Dachau

5353 Magnolia St. Phila. 44, Pa.
April 5, 1961

Inquirer
400 N. Broad St., Philadelphia, Pa.

To the Editor:

Bob Considine in his third series on "Horror and Death at Dachau" (April 5) quotes Auxiliary Bishop of Munich, Johann Neuhaeusler. In it Mr. Considine quotes a character as saying that they will "kick us into the gas chamber" giving the customary impression that Dachau gassed thousands to death.

Way back on August 27, 1949, Bishop Neuhaeusler in an interview he granted me in Munich made it clear that **nobody was gassed to death at Dachau.** He has since also stated this in his booklet, **"So war es in Dachau."** (G. Manz AG., Munich, 72 pages, DM 2.50).

The facts seem to be that a total of 206,000 prisoners, some political but also many real criminals experienced Dachau between 1933 and 1945. Of these a maximum of 27,000 did not come out alive, some done to death, others dying from other causes mostly of typhus, which compares roughly with the American prisoners of war who were done to death or died during the Civil War in the one prisoner-of-war camp of Andersonville, under the auspices of fellow Americans.

In matters of atrocities, if one is honorable, one will make very sure of the facts and will also keep atrocities in perspective with those of other nations.

Yours truly,

Austin J. App, Ph.D.

—————————•♦•—————————

(105)

Nisei and Jews Treated as "Potential Enemies"

5353 Magnolia St., Phila. 44, Pa.
August 9, 1961

Time
Rockefeller Center
New York 20, N.Y.

Sir:

Those who want historical as well as material justice for all the participants in World War II will be deeply grateful to you for your story "20

Years After" of the internment of 110,000 West Coast Japanese.   (Aug. 11 issue.)

Now that many use the Eichmann trial to perpetuate the indictment of the German people, one may suggest that the American people as a whole realized as little of this anti-Japanese crime as the German people claim to have realized their government's anti-Jewish crimes.

Furthermore our wartime government justified its putting the Nisei—men, women, and children—into concentration camps on the basis of their being potential enemies. Similarly Eichmann testified that in as much as world Jewish organizations had even formally declared war on Germany, he felt justified in sending European Jews into concentration camps as "potential enemies."

Whether if Japan had succeeded in invading the West Coast and obliterating our cities with bombs, our government would have finally resorted to executing Nisei the way the German government executed Jews during the years of impending defeat, only God, literally only God can know! Certainly, Walter Lippmann, whom you quote, and others like him, have good reason to think twice before calling for a continued barrage of stones at the German people.

Respectfully yours,

A. J. App, Ph.D.

━━━●●━━━

(106)

Oder-Neisse Lands not America's to Give Away

August 10, 1961

Wall Street Journal
44 Broad St., New York

Sir:

Having been a guest of honor at the rally of 300,000 Silesians in Hannover June 10-11, where both Adenauer and Brandt assured these Oder-Neisse expellees that the right to their homelands and to self-determination is sacred, I heartily endorse your editorial "No Solution in Sorcery" (Aug. 10), in which you discourage our making the Oder-Neisse line permanent, in exchange for Soviet promises in Berlin.

Our conceding the Oder-Neisse lands to the Soviets would be a monstrous injustice. But more than that: those lands do not belong to us. They belong to the people who for 900 years were settled in these lands. Only they could validly cede them to Russia or Poland. We may not do so, and even Bonn may not do it. Only the Silesians I saw this summer, and the East Prussians and Pomeranians may do it. And' they will not do it, as little as Californians would give up California to China or Russia—just to make it easy for some politicians to shrug off stupidities like those committed at Yalta and Potsdam.

Sincerely yours,

A. J. App, Ph.D.
LaSalle College

— 97 —

Liberal Catholics and Communism

August 10, 1961

The National Review
150 East 35th Street
New York 16, N.Y.

Sir:

As a Catholic college graduate and professor, I want to compliment L. Brent Bozell on his handling of a difficult topic in "The Strange Drift of Liberal Catholicism."

Just when Catholicism in America is emerging from its minority complexes into respectability, it is suffering from a widening rift between, for want of better words, conservatism and "liberalism."

It became evident in the debates between interventionism and non-interventionism before Pearl Harbor. Those who strongly favored intervention "in a war to end all wars" went along with Unconditional Surrender and acquiesced in Morgenthauism, and the betrayals of Yalta and Potsdam.

These made Soviet Russia the monstrous master of much of Europe and Asia. The conservatives feel free to blame communist and left wing influences in America for these sell-outs. But the "liberals", not yet chastened enough to admit their having been deceived, want to justify themselves by blaming the communistic victories on hunger and bad housing in various parts of the globe!

One can confidently assume, however, that when the chips will be down, when the ultimate show-down with the communist conspiracy will have to be faced, the so-called liberal Catholics will move firmly to the right. They may even come to throw a few belated bouquets at McCarthy!

Yours truly,

A. J. App, Ph.D.

Lippmann Blames Hitler for Yalta Sell-Outs

November 5, 1961

Inquirer, Phila., Pa.

To the Editor:

On Oct. 31, your columnist Walter Lippmann, calling the partition of Germany a regrettable status quo, continues,

> *"But if anyone is to be blamed it is Hitler, who started the war and lost it."*

That sort of soothing **alibi-ing** won't do! One might just as logically blame Martin Luther for the Seven Years War—or Almighty God for Original Sin! No, with Unconditional Surrender, Hitler and Germany were effectively relieved of all responsibility for the subsequent crimes and blunders of peace making. The criminal expulsions of Germans from the Oder-Neisse lands and the disgraceful partitioning of Germany are the direct, provable fruits of Morgenthauism and the Yalta-Potsdam pacts deriving from this policy of vengeance.

The Lord who said, "Vengeance is mine" may blame Hitler for many wrongs, but for the partition of Germany after Unconditional Surrender His wrath will fall on those who now have cause to invent alibis. What is wrong with the likes of Lippmann is that they still try to keep alive World War II against Germany rather than bestir themselves in the Cold War against Soviet Russia. That also explains why America and the Free World keep on losing!

Respectfully yours,

A. J. App, Ph.D.

———————•◦•———————

(109)

Soft-on-Communism Line is Widespread

December 26, 1961

Times Chronicle
Jenkintown, Pa.

To the Editor:

As one of the speakers on the Ideas of Liberty program in Abington on November 30, 1961, I want to thank the *Times Chronicle* for its publicity and the patriotic sense of the community for sponsoring such a program. Its purpose was to promote the American free enterprise system, to warn against the dangers of communism at home, and to urge resistance to communist appeasement in Europe.

The need for such programs is eloquently illustrated by the warped comments on it by Correspondent Edward Schempp (Dec. 14, 1961). His whole letter amounts to a snide attack on the principle of private property and a sly apology for socialism, if not communism.

Because I demanded an end to Soviet appeasement in Europe and a just peace for Germany based on the principles of the Atlantic Charter, which barred such territorial transfers as the Oder-Neisse lands to the Soviets, he would call me "a lobbyist of Germany." Pretending to champion the "sacred rights of the individual", he gets angry when I expose the expulsion by the Soviets of ten million Germans from the Oder-Neisse lands, the brutal murder of two million of them, and total robbery of all of them! Persons who sanction such wholesale confiscation of private property and who would appease Soviet Russia with the Oder-Neisse territories and who would smear anyone who wants Communist crimes treated exactly as Nazi crimes, such persons are witting or unwitting promoters of the Communist line! I say this seriously and absolutely.

Mr. Schempp's whole letter is full of typical sneers against "the sacred rights of property," against those who are "completely against Communism," who consider "even a little socialism dangerous." He refers sarcastically to "the rules God has given the elite for the handling of Communists"! Clearly, the existence of such soft-on-communism types is sufficient proof that more anti-Communist libertarian programs are needed. More power to those who sponsor them.

Respectfully,

A. J. App, Ph.D.

———————•◦•———————

(110)

Keeping the Maps of Germany Correct

March 7, 1962

Inquirer, Philadelphia, Pa.

Dear Sir:

Your feature, "World's Trouble Spots" with the map of Germany was most interesting.

But in such future maps of Germany would you please show Germany

— 99 —

in its proper boundaries as specified in the Potsdam pact, pending the final peace treaty.

East Germany—the provinces of Silesia, Pomerania, Southern East Prussia—is only under Polish administration. These provinces are no more a part of Poland than the Soviet Zone of Germany is a part of Russia. It is very important that the subtle pro-Soviet propaganda suggested by such misleading maps be avoided.

Yours respectfully,

A. J. App, Ph.D.
LaSalle College

(111)

Expulsions Best Proof of German Character of the Oder-Neisse Lands

November 12, 1962

Brooklyn *Tablet*
One Hanson Place
Brooklyn, N.Y.

To the Editor:

In his letter on the Oder-Neisse territories Mr. Kusielewicz writes that "Poles completely inhabit and control these lands today," and he has "never heard of a single inhabitant of the territories east of the Oder-Neisse Line demanding his return to Germany."

Of course not. The ten million German-speaking inhabitants of those lands were brutally expelled in 1945, some two million of them killed. The mere fact that they had to be expelled to put these lands under Polish administration is bloody enough proof of their German character.

These expulsions were the most enormous crime of World War II, larger in scale than the worst of Hitler's. Anyone who claims these lands for Poland because hundreds of years ago Poland allegedly controlled them plays right into the plots of the Communists, who are just waiting to have Mexico claim all of our American Southwest, which has been in American hands at best only half as long as the Oder-Neisse lands have been, not only under German control, but completely German in speech and culture. Their expulsion was a crime that must be made retrogressive by the full return of these lands to the people who were expelled from them.

Respectfully yours,

A. J. App, Ph.D.
LaSalle College
(President, Federation of
American Citizens of German Descent)

(112)

The Six Million Figure is a Smear-Terrorizing Myth

June 29, 1965

Time Magazine
Times Square, New York
229 W. 43rd Street

To the Editor:

As a Milwaukee-born American of German descent and a college teacher of literature, I want to compliment you on your marvelous summary article entitled, "The German Awakening." It was far more honest and objective than a victor customarily writes about the vanquished.

Nevertheless two items require comment. One is that the Nazi leadership "moved from the false premises to the insanely logical conclusion of systematic extermination." There is not one single document, order, blueprint, or "Morgenthau Plan," to support the statement that the Nazis planned the extermination of the Jews. Their so-called end solution of trying to squeeze them out of Germany is not extermination, as the Czechs and the Poles who expelled 15,000,000 East and Sudeten Germans, with Stalin-Churchill-Roosevelt approval, would be the first to insist.

That they did not plan extermination of all Jews under occupation is obvious from the fact that they **did not** exterminate them. Every Jew who survived the German occupation is proof of this. The Nazis were so efficient that not a calf was born without their record nor a pig slaughtered. Had they determined to kill all Jews, they would have done so— they had five years to do it in.

The second point is President Heinrich Luebke's allegedly speaking of "6,000,000 Jews who were murdered." Have you proof that he said this? If he did he gives pathetic evidence of the power of smear tactics to foist a propaganda lie on the world. There is ten times more evidence that the number of Jews the Nazis executed for right or wrong reasons is a quarter of a million, about the number of German women and children and wounded who died in the bloody attack on Dresden, than that it is six million. Tragic and criminal enough—but Dresden was tragic, too, and perjuring historical truth is criminal, too!

The first duty of the victor toward the vanquished is the truth. It is a pity that President Luebke felt he had to echo that libel in order not to be smear-terrorized.

Yours truly,

A. J. App, Ph.D.

NOTE:—On the same day a reply was sent to a Jewish correspondent who had sent the writer the *Time* essay with his own comments. Dr. App's reply contains the following paragraph:

"We Germans all over the world, whether by nationality or by descent, have an almost pitiable desire to be friends with the Jewish people. BUT whenever some obvious vindictiveness on the part of Jews and Communists explodes or some obvious propaganda exaggeration like the myth of the six millions we feel slapped in the face—and it is our duty to protest, even for the sake of the Jews—for the longer they keep alive the six million myth by chiefly smear tactics—calling anyone an anti-Semite who questions it—the more the wrath of those deceived will someday be."

(113)

German Expellees Want Homelands Back

July 11, 1963

Time Magazine
Time and Life Building
Rockefeller Center
New York 20, N.Y.

To the Editor:

Just returned from Europe and catching up on my *Time,* I was pleased with your full account (June 20 issue) of the mass reunion of Silesian expellees in Cologne. Your reference to "one of the worst forced migrations of modern times, 9,400,000 ethnic Germans . . . abruptly expelled" is perfect. But reporting the Silesians as "Germans expelled from Communist Poland after World War II" is misleading. They were expelled from an ancient and solid part of Germany by Soviet-directed Poles!

Also, as one who sat on the stage during the rally, may I suggest that reporting that "the **gemütlich** scene suddenly turned into a riot" gives a totally false picture. No tomatoes were thrown, no fists flew. The crowd concertedly, somewhat rhythmically, but not raucously, demanded, " 'Raus mit DuMont" (Let DuMont get out) until a few policemen non-forcibly escorted him off the stage. To make that sound like one of our own bloody racial riots is false.

But what most urgently needs correction is your suggestion that the German demand for the restoration of the Oder-Neisse homelands to the expellees is "becoming increasingly hollow." It is not! It is becoming more grass roots and insistent than ever. And the more the world palavers about international justice, the more it insists on self-determination for even the most backward colonial peoples, the more the rank-and-file Germans are bewildered as to how such a professedly **just** world can think of denying such self-determination to the 9,400,000 expellees and can for one moment consider ratifying the monstrous crime of the expulsions by settling their robbed homelands on the expulsionists!

Do let me assure you, seventy million Germans, despite some well-publicized hirelings, if not outright Red subversives, will want an Atlantic Charter justice in this matter. To suggest otherwise is to do much eventual harm.

Respectfully yours,

A. J. App, Ph.D.
LaSalle College, Phila.

———◄●►———

(114)

The Story of the Crucifixion is not Anti-Semitic

June 15, 1964

Rev. John B. Sheerin, C.S.P.
Editor, *The Catholic World*
411 W. 59th Street
New York City, N.Y.
Dear Father Sheerin:

I read with interest your vigorous column, "Council Statement on Jews" (*Catholic Standard and Times*, June 12, 1964).

You urge the official Church to renounce once and forever the big lie on which anti-Semitism is based—the lie that "the Jewish race is guilty of the murder of Christ."

While the historical and biblical truth is that the Jews crucified Christ, and not for example as our movie makers keep trying to suggest that it was the Romans (Italians) who did it, it seems incomprehensible that any Christian would hold Jews today responsible or guilty of what their alleged ancestors did 2000 years ago.

Can so-called anti-Semitism be said to derive in this way? Certainly Father Leonard Feeney, who was denounced as an anti-Semite, could not possibly be so illogical and untheological as to blame modern Jews for the crime of their ancestors centuries ago!

He was denounced as an anti-Semite because he protested the efforts of important Jewish forces to-day of trying to get Christ out of Christmas, prayers out of schools, and rejecting and opposing Christ generally. He was denounced because he refused to imitate Peter when he denied Christ three times.

What can the Council do about persons like Feeney? Would a Council statement really touch the problem?

— 102 —

I consider it the most difficult one in our time for any true Christian. I take the liberty of inclosing a sheet which quotes the recently deceased and never repudiated Jewish spokesman Ben Hecht on the Crucifixion. And a pamphlet on "Anti-Semitism a Phoney Bogey."

Very respectfully yours,

Austin J. App, Ph.D.

(115)

Retiring Editor of THE WANDERER a Giant of Right Thinking

January 18, 1964

The Wanderer
128 E. Tenth Street
St. Paul 1, Minn.

Gentlemen:

I am reading in your increasingly wonderful and necessary paper that after sixty-six years Mr. Joseph Matt is retiring as editor and promoting his son Walter L. Matt to that responsibility.

Mr. Matt's retiring makes me sad on two counts: It registers the passage of time for him, and me, and all of us. When I first met him, during the difficult war years, he seemed to be about my age now. His best work then seemed to begin as did Adenauers—at an age when most of us already decline! His retiring makes me personally feel old.

Secondly, his retiring marks the muting of a giant of Christian conservatism and journalistic righteousness. Like John the Baptist, he raised a mighty voice for policies that should have been—but were not! He retires on a world in which the evil policies of Morgenthauism and Communist appeasement and anti-Christianity have brought America and Europe to what seems to me (who know history fairly well) to the worst pass in literally 1900 years. I am sorry to see Mr. Matt Senior subside when what looks to me like the final show-down is approaching rapidly.

I am of course confident that what is Christian in America and Europe will arouse itself in time and sufficiently to triumph ultimately, however bludgeoned. One reason for this confidence is that more and more young Americans, and Germans, and Englishmen, and West Europeans generally are taking up the gauntlet for truth, justice, and godliness.

Distinguished among these is Walter Matt, the son who is stepping into his father's mighty shoes as editor. I wish him much joy and much luck. Whether God has given him the encyclopedic knowledge that has always astounded me in his father. I do not know. But I do know that he has the same sense of truth and justice and honor. May the *Wanderer* thrive under his editorship and may the father long keep a guiding eye on it.

As professor of literature in a Catholic college and the president of the Federation of American Citizens of German Descent, I felt strongly like writing this.

Sincerely yours,

Austin J. App, Ph.D.

— 103 —

Hunt All War Criminals — or None

5353 Magnolia St., Phila. 44, Pa.
January 23, 1965

The *Inquirer*
Phila., Pa., 19101

To the Edtior:

In your editorial "Keep the 'Nazi Hunt' Going" (January 23, 1965) you urge the West German Parliament "to extend the statute of Limitations on trying Nazi murderers for 10 more years," so that, among other reasons, the Soviet Union and its "satellite yelpers" can no longer use the issue for its "stream of abuse."

Would it not be more proper to urge the Reds to make a start on prosecuting their own war criminals, instead of presuming to call for more West German trials?

The world has no right to discriminate among war criminals! The victors and their satellites have absolutely no moral right to treat the war criminals of the vanquished nations more harshly than they are prepared to treat their own!

For twenty years now, first we victors directly, then the Germans by our directives, have been prosecuting and executing German war criminals.

In the meanwhile, what have the victors done about their own war criminals? Who has called for the prosecution of the Russians who murdered 11,000 Polish officers at Katyn (and at Nuremberg tried to blame the Nazis for it!)? When will those Czechs be prosecuted who expelled and robbed 3,000,000 Sudetens and murdered some 250,000 of them? When will those Poles be prosecuted who expelled and robbed nine million Oder-Neisse Germans and did to death nearly a million of them?

When will the Soviet officers and men be prosecuted who raped a million German women and children? Or the Allied airmen who, after razing German cities, went on to snipe to death fleeing German women and children (as at Dresden)?

On January 14, you report, 250 pickets "from a number of Jewish organizations" protested at the German consulate "over West Germany's refusal to extend the statute of limitations on Nazi war criminals" (Inquirer, Jan. 15)! Have those pickets demanded that Israel prosecute the Jews guilty of the Der Yassin massacre of Arabs, or the Israeli statesmen who with those of France and Britain committed the act of aggression against Egypt in 1956, every bit as criminal as Hitler's attack on Poland in 1939?

Let us emphasize: It is our moral duty not to discriminate among war criminals but to treat those of all nations and parties and races by the same standards! If we want to keep on hunting war criminals, let us be absolutely clear about this, morality and gentlemanliness require that we hunt all war criminals alike, not just the Nazis. Otherwise our very discrimination in the matter makes us war criminals psychologically!

Yours truly,

Austin J. App, Ph.D.

(117)

Baruch was a Vindictive Morgenthauist

July 11, 1965

National Review
150 E. 35th Street
New York 16, N.Y.

To the Editor:

In your editorial, "Bernard M. Baruch, RIP," you charitably speak of Baruch as having belonged to the class we might call "the good citizen." You speak of his poise and serenity. I, too, recall this as he one day sauntered toward the grandstand during the Steuben Day parade.

But this every poise made him when he was wrong all the more effective for evil. Baruch was vindictive towards the German people, one of the chief sponsors of the Morgenthau plan, the most vicious peace plan in Christian history. The N.Y. *Times* on June 23, 1945, had the following headline: "Baruch says Peace Depends on Ending Reich's War Power; Her Heavy Industry Should be Removed or Destroyed, He Tells Senate Group."

In a fourteen point program of "what is to be done with Germany," he parallels the disastrous Morgenthau plan:

> "Break once and for all Germany's dominance of Europe. Her war-making potential must be eliminated; many of her plants and factories shifted east and west to friendly countries, all other heavy industries destroyed; the Junkers' estates broken up; her exports and imports strictly controlled. German assets and business organizations all over the world rooted out."

There would be no Volkswagens about had Baruch's ideas prevailed!

Worse than the above, for a man who professed democratic principles, he favored labor slavery for the German people:

> "Russia and other countries are entitled to labor reparations, particularly if they will include in their battalions the principle war makers, the Nazis, the Gestapo, Junkers, the Generalstaff, geopolitikers, war industrialists, war financiers, leaving the ordinary peasant and workers."

This is the Morgenthau line; it is also the Communistic line! And it also must be insisted that any German who could have been proved to have projected such a plan for Germany's enemies would have been hanged as a war criminal—and should have been!

Yours truly,

Austin J. App, Ph.D.
LaSalle College

---

(118)

Why Must Leftist Poet Spender be Given Library of Congress Sinecure

October 5, 1965

Human Events
410 First Street, S.E.
Washington 3, D.C.

To the Editor:

Ralph de Toledano's article on Stephen Spender entitled, "Left-Wing British Poet named to Library of Congress Post" happily threw the spotlight on an appointment that warrants scrutiny.

Why was precisely this particular British second-rate poet appointed to the honorable post once held by Robert Frost?

The sympathetic **Twentieth Century Authors** describes this **British** author as "On his mother's side. . . . . . partly German, partly Jewish descent." It says flatly that "By the time he had left the university, Spender, like Auden and Lewis, had proclaimed himself a Communist." It adds that "it is doubtful, however, whether he has ever joined the Communist Party, and some of his views would certainly be considered heretical in Moscow."

Why must a one-time self-proclaimed Communist, who, even if he were never to have carried a card, certainly never proclaimed western ideals of democracy either, be appointed to the most distinguished literary sinecure the U. S. has to offer?

Respectfully yours,

Austin J. App, Ph.D.
LaSalle College, Phila.

————————◆•◆————————

(119)

Contrasting Welch on Eisenhower with the Liberals on Goldwater

November 9, 1965

Wall Street Journal
1015—14th Street, N.W.
Washington, D.C., 20005

To the Editor:

When Communists attack Robert Welch I am glad; when the *Wall Street Journal*, my favorite paper, and William Henry Chamberlin, courageous author of **America's 2nd Crusade**, write, "John Birch Society No Help to Conservatism" (Nov. 9), I am sad.

So far every anti-Communist protagonist was finally destroyed—Martin Dies, Father Coughlin, Senator McCarthy, James Forrestal. All of them, before their anti-Communism really hurt the conspiracy, were respected for their talent, character, and idealism, and had support from high and low. Thereafter, their smallest failings were escalated until finally their staunchest supporters had been induced to turn gravediggers.

The recent turning upon Robert Welch by Chamberlin, Buckley, and Senator Dodd simply charts the ominous pattern when the satanic apparatus is beginning to succeed in trapping honest conservatives into doing their dirty work for them. When will honorable anti-communists grasp the fact that the power of iniquity can vilify any man, presented even the Son of God so that finally most of his followers and one of his Apostles turned against him?

Against Welch virtually the only charge boils down to his having called Eisenhower "a dedicated, conscious agent of the Communist conspiracy?" But has anyone called for the elimination from public life of all those liberals who in 1964 with no justification at all likened Barry Goldwater to Hitler, an infinitely more harmful and irresponsible association?

As regards Eisenhower, the fact remains that he did give express approval to the Morgenthau Plan, the most genocidic document in Christian history. Even Secretary of State Hull said it would exterminate thirty million Germans! And the chief miseries now—the division of Germany, the Wall, the Iron Curtain—all stem from this plan which Eisenhower approved—and implemented to that point and until some of us like General Patton, Herbert Hoover, Robert Taft, and also William Henry Chamberlin, got it belatedly modified.

THAT PLAN was drafted by Communist Harry Dexter White and sponsored by Henry Morgenthau, Jr. It betrayed half of Christian Europe to the Red slavery and prepared the way for betraying China. Eisenhower explicitly approved this plan. He therefore was as a plain matter of fact an agent, presumably of course an unwitting one, of the Communist conspiracy. But whether he was a "conscious one" only he could know—and as far as I know he has not told us!

CERTAINLY I do not think him a "conscious" agent. I feel quite sure that he stood in relation to the Morgenthau Plan only as Pontius Pilate stood in relation to the Good Friday tragedy—he was in one way or another pressured into approval. But until he himself tells us so, as Pontius Pilate told us, one cannot absolutely call Welch wrong in thinking Eisenhower "a conscious agent". For Eisenhower did in fact, in harmony with Red blueprints, apply to conquered Europe the pro-Communistic Morgenthau Plan which lost the peace and precipitated the cold war.

Anyhow, until all liberals who likened Goldwater to Hitler have been crucified, it is thoroughly improper and inexpedient to crucify Robert Welch for having pointed up Eisenhower's complicity with the genocidic Morgenthau Plan. And I respect Eisenhower enough to assume he would agree!

Yours truly,

Austin J. App, PhD.

Christian Formula for a Good Peace

(During the some five years of the tragic decade from 1941 to 1951, which perverted the Atlantic Charter ideal into the Morgenthau Plan and the Yalta and Potsdam betrayals into "history's most terrifying peace," the author had printed on his envelopes under the return address the formula here used to conclude this collection of Morgenthau Era letters.)

Only a just peace is a good peace.
Only a just peace deserves to last.
God demands of us a just peace.

He does not want of us an **enforced,** or **guaranteed,** or **secure** peace: an enforced peace is a gangster's ideal; a guaranteed peace is a presumption and illusion; and a secure peace is the prerogative and gift of God to "Men of Good Will."

To enforce, guarantee, or secure an **unjust** peace is a crime.
Robbing territories, expelling people, partitioning and de-industrializing countries, slave-labor reparations are criminal injustices.

"Men of Good Will" do to the Vanquished what they if vanquished would want done to themselves.

Concluding Comment (added Dec. 1, 1965)

Twenty years after cessation of hostilities, after German Unconditional Surrender, itself an atrocity, there is still no peace treaty with Germany. The self-proclaimed "peace-loving" Big Three, who arrogated to themselves the right to **dictate** and **enforce** everlasting peace, promptly fell out amongst themselves, like typical gangsters, and have been in a Cold War ever since. The reason for this tragedy, the end of which is not yet, is that the Morgenthauistic and treasonable elements that dominated our publicity channels and official Washington violated every one of the axioms in the above FORMULA to the grim advantage of Soviet Russia, the most totalitarian and brutal empire in history, the only one that has erected walls and barbed wire entanglements, not to keep the foe **out,** but its own people **in.**

May these humble letters be the widow's mite to get the country back to Atlantic Charter principles before the Yalta betrayals will have been consummated in a Third World War!

BIOGRAPHICAL NOTES

A. J. App, Ph.D., in Response to *Modern Language Association* "The Association Goes to War" Circular and Questionnaire — May 19, 1948

In September, 1942, I was drafted from my position as head of the English department at the University of Scranton, Scranton, Pennsylvania, and became an army engineer, doing three months of basic training at Fort Belvoir, Virginia. Then I was transferred to Camp Claiborne, Louisiana, serving as secretary in the Inspector General's Office. In March 1943 I was honorably discharged to become administrative assistant to the personnel manager of a war plant, The Jaeger Machine Company, Columbus, Ohio.

SPECIAL NOTE: *I do not mind recounting my services during the war, and I think it is also well for the Association collectively to do it and to put on record, but only on one condition, namely that the Association recognize that the American government has consistently tried to hang as war criminals all those Germans, including very particularly also all those German scholars and professors, who during the war served their country and government in the way the Association now tries to record that American scholars and professors served this country and government in the total war effort, that the Association recognize that this government has in fact hanged some Germans for doing what it is intended to record that members of the Association did, and that therefore this Association make strong representation to the government of the United States that it either stop trying to hang Germans for having helped their country's war effort or the members of this Association will in any future war consider themselves bound to act towards the government and the country's war effort exactly as this Morgenthauistic government is asserting that Germans should have acted, which is that they should rather let themselves be executed as traitors than to have aided the war effort!*

I strongly and seriously urge the officers of the Modern Language Association to make some such representation to the members of our government and our military, and to put some such comment in the preface of the proposed record.

Respectfully submitted,

Austin J. App, Ph.D.
Professor, Incarnate Word College
San Antonio, Texas

SUPPLEMENTAL BIOGRAPHICAL DATA:
(Added Nov. 27, 1965)

The author of these letters was born in Milwaukee, grew up on a farm near Lake Michigan, and got an A.B. degree from St. Francis Seminary, Milwaukee. He won a Knights of Columbus graduate fellowship to the Catholic University, Washington, D.C., got an M.A. in 1926, and a Ph.D. in English in 1929. He taught there until 1935, when he became head of the English department of the University of Scranton. Also, because of his congeniality to them, he was designated to conduct a special Bible history course for the Jewish students.

After the war he taught at Incarnate Word College until 1948, and thereafter at LaSalle College, Philadelphia, where he is associate professor of English. From 1949 to 1959, he was chairman of the Pastorius Unit No. 38 of the Steuben Society. In 1961 he became national president of the Federation of American Citizens of German Descent; in 1963 he was made an Honorary Member of D.A.N.K.; in 1964, chairman of the Greater Philadelphia Captive Nations Committee; in 1965, chairman of the Philadelphia Committee to Support Your Local Police. He was co-founder in 1954 and since then chairman of the Philadelphia Catholic Poetry Society. In 1965 he became the President of the Pennsylvania Chapter of the International Committee for the Defence of Christian Culture.

He has traveled, lectured and written much. Has criss-crossed Western Europe ten summers, given talks there and in most states at home, has written hundreds of reviews and articles, many pamphlets, and eight books, including such titles as *History's Most Terrifying Peace* (1946), *Way to Creative Writing* (1954), and *Making the Later Years Count* (1960). He is an elected member of the Gallery of Living Catholic Authors. He is not married, a Roman Catholic, means to get to heaven, but not before the Morgenthauists are elsewhere, and Germany is re-united in its proper boundaries, and the Captive Nations are liberated!

Index of Personal Names

Adams, John — 2
Adenauer, Dr. Konrad — 82, 87, 97, 193
Alexander, Holmes — 94
Allers, Dr. Rudolf — 25
Arnold, Benedict — 1
Arnold, General Henry H. — 86
Ascham, Roger — 10
Attlee, Prime Minister C. L. — 76
Auden, Wystan Hugh — 106
Baer, Herman — 90
Barth, Karl — 69
Baruch, Bernard M. — 54, 58, 68, 105
Beaconsfield, Lord — 48
Beard, Dr. Charles A. — 72
Beran, Msgr. Joseph — 78
Bernadotte, Count — 85
Bess, Demaree — 23
Bismarck, Chancellor Otto von — 85
Binsse, H. L. — 30
Bleibtreu, Adolf — 81
Boland, Congressman Patrick J. — 6
Bozell, L. Brent — 98
Bradley, General Omar Nelson — 86
Brandt, Willy — 62, 63, 97
Braun, Wernher von — 94
Bricker, Senator John W. — 87
Bruening, Dr. Heinrich — 51
Buck, Pearl — 11
Buckley, William F. — 106
Bullitt, William C. — 29
Burke, Edmund — 22
Byers, Cary — 47
Byrnes, Secretary James F. — 71
Cain, Senator Harry Pulliam — 82, 87
Chamberlin, William Henry — 69, 106
Capehart, Senator Homer E. — 87
Chapman, Emanuel — 50
Christ Our Lord — 31, 54, 102, 106
Churchill, Prime Minister —
    5, 8, 15, 24, 25, 39, 43, 59
Clancy, William P. — 87
Clapper, Columnist Raymond — 8
Cogley, Journalist John — 87
Colby, Frank — 19
Considine, Bob — 96
Coughlin, Father Charles — 106
Cowan, A. — 50
Crawford, Ollie — 77
Davies, Joseph E. — 12, 13, 19
Davis, Elmer — 12
Dewey, Governor Thomas E. — 42, 73, 74, 76
DeWitt, General J. L. — 63
Diem, President Ngo Dinh — 16
Dies, Congressman Martin — 106
Dirksen, Senator Everett M. — 87
Dodd, Senator Thomas J. — 106
Dos Passos, John — 89
Dulles, Secretary John Foster — 90, 93
DuMont, Neven Juergen — 102
Eichmann, Adolf — 95, 96, 97
Einstein, Albert — 64
Eisenhower, General Dwight D. —
    33, 36, 57, 59, 86, 87, 106, 107
Eisler, Gearhart — 77, 78
Eyck, Erich — 85
Faulhaber, Cardinal Michael von — 58, 71
Faulkner, William — 89
Feeney, Father Leonard — 102
Fenton, Father Joseph Clifford — 91
Fish, Congressman Hamilton — 15, 73
Flossdorf, Rev. Augustin — 85
Forrest, General Nathan B. — 94
Forrestall, Secretary James — 106
Franco, General Francisco — 53, 56, 60, 80
Frost, Robert — 105
Furfey, Msgr. Paul Hanly — 60
Gallico, Paul — 32, 33
Gardiner, Alexander — 32, 34
Gardiner, Rev. Harold C. — 61
Gideonse, Dr. Harry D. — 72
Gillis, Editor James Martin—82, 92
God the Father — 35, 93
Goering, Herman — 59
Goethe, Wolfgang von — 35
Gold, Michael — 89
Goldwater, Barry — 106, 107
Gollancz, Victor — 73

Grew, Ambassador Joseph C. — 16
Griffin, Archbishop — 59
Guffey, Senator Joseph F. — 6
Gurion, Ben — 84
Halsey, Admiral William F. — 49, 50
Hanser, Richard — 72
Hatch, Robert L. — 10, 11
Hazlitt, Henry — 90
Hecht, Ben — 68, 103
Hemingway, Ernest — 89
Herman, Prof. F. A. — 46
Hershey, Bernet — 46
Hitler, Adolf — 1, 2, 5, 6, 7, 8, 9, 13, 14, 21, 22, 35,
    37, 52, 53, 54, 55, 59, 63, 69, 79, 85, 86, 98, 100
Hocking, William Ernest — 35
Hoettl, Dr. Wilhelm — 79
Hoover, President Herbert — 107
Housman, Laurence — 46
Hull, Secretary Cordell — 6, 24, 73, 87, 107
Hurley, Bishop Joseph Patrick — 4
Hutchins, Robert M. — 54
Inge, Dean William Ralph — 83
Jackson, General Stonewall — 94
Jefferson, Thomas — 2
Jenner, Senator William E. — 87
John the Baptist — 103
Journet, Father Charles — 91
Judas Iscariot — 50
Kaiser Wilhelm II — 3, 21
Kazda, Matilda — 79
Kazin, Alfred — 53
Kenkel, F. P. — 54
Knowles, Arthur J. — 50
Knox, Secretary Frank — 4, 6, 15, 16
Koch, Ilse — 74, 75, 78
Krock, Arthur — 2, 4
Krueger, General Walter — 33, 36, 43, 64, 68
Kuehnelt-Leddihn, Erik V. — 73
Kusielewicz — 100
LaFollette, Senator Robert M. — 35
Langer, Senator William — 81, 87
Lansing, Secretary Robert — 80
Lawrence, David — 68
Lee, General Robert E. — 94
Lewis, C. Day — 106
Lewis, Dr. William Draper — 58
Lincoln, President Abraham — 33, 35
Lindbergh, Col. Charles — 2, 15, 37
Lippmann, Walter — 97, 98
Luce, Clare Booth — 42, 63
Ludwig, Emil — 60, 61, 64, 68
Luebke, President Heinrich — 101
Luther, Martin — 98
McCarran, Senator Pat — 87
McCarthy, Senator Joseph — 87, 98, 106
Mackay, Charles — 21, 22
Mann, Thomas — 26
Marshall, C. N. — 80
Marshall, General George C. — 86
Matt, Editor Joseph — 103
Matt, Walter L. — 103
Mayer, Milton — 68
Meier, Minister Golda — 69
Millikan, Dr. Robert A. — 18, 19
Mises, Ludwig von — 85
Morgenthau, Jr., Secretary Henry —
    24, 40, 41, 53, 58, 60, 61, 68, 107
Morrison, Charles Clayton — 68
Muench, Bishop Alousius J. — 56
Mussolini, Benito — 53, 89
Nasser, Gamal Abdel — 89
Neuhäusler, Bishop Johann — 96
Niemoeller, Pastor Martin — 58
Nimitz, Admiral Chester Wm. — 33, 36, 43
Oesterreicher, Msgr. John M. — 91
O'Gara, James — 87
Paassen, Pierre van — 7, 8
Padover, Saul K. — 63
Patton, General George S. — 86, 107
Peter the Apostle — 102
Peterman, Ivan H. — 86
Pfeifer, Congressman Joseph — 80
Pontius Pilate — 107
Pope Pius XI — 84
Pope Pius XII — 26, 31, 55, 65, 77
Poullada, Leon B. — 75
Prescott, Orville — 22